GODS OF THE ANCIENT WORLD

A KIDS' GUIDE TO ANCIENT MYTHOLOGIES

WRITTEN BY MARCHELLA WARD

Editor Satu Hämeenaho-Fox
Designer Lisa Robb
Project Editor Rosie Peet
Senior Designer Nathan Martin
Production Editor Siu Yin Chan
Senior Production Controller Louise Minihane
Senior Picture Researcher Sakshi Saluja
Senior Acquisitions Editor Katy Flint
Managing Art Editor Vicky Short
Publishing Director Mark Searle

Written by Marchella Ward
Illustrated by Xuan Le

For QZA—thank you for sharing your God with me.
Chella

First American Edition, 2023
Published in the United States by DK Publishing
1745 Broadway, 20th Floor, New York, NY 10019

Page design copyright © 2023 Dorling Kindersley
Limited
A Division of Penguin Random House LLC
Text copyright © Marchella Ward, 2023
Artwork copyright © Xuan Le, 2023

23 24 25 26 27   10 9 8 7 6 5 4 3 2 1
001–331552–Feb/23

A catalog record for this book is available from the
Library of Congress.
ISBN 978-0-7440-6096-6

DK books are available at special discounts
when purchased in bulk for sales promotions,
premiums, fund-raising, or educational use.
For details, contact: DK Publishing Special Markets,
1745 Broadway, 20th Floor, New York, NY 10019
SpecialSales@dk.com

Printed and bound in Slovakia.

For the curious
www.dk.com

This book is made from
Forest Stewardship Council™
certified paper—one small
step in DK's commitment
to a sustainable future.

GODS
OF THE
ANCIENT
WORLD

A KIDS' GUIDE TO ANCIENT MYTHOLOGIES

CONTENTS

RULERS OF NATURE

KEEPING HUMANS IN LINE

WHY DO HUMANS TELL STORIES?

For as long as there have been humans, we have tried to understand the world around us. Myths, folktales, and legends are part of how we make sense of the world. Gods and goddesses, humans and animals, monsters and demons were more than just characters in these stories. They were how ancient people answered some of life's biggest questions, many of which are still mysterious to us today. How exactly did the world come to be? Can good overcome evil? Why are some people luckier than others?

Stories turn up in interesting places. We find them in the voices of storytellers, crumpled between the pages of library books, boxed up in dark basement archives, scratched underneath the objects in museums, and half-remembered by our grandparents and great-grandparents. They come to us when we are looking for them, as well as when we aren't. The stories in this book come from all across the ancient world, including cultures that many people don't get taught about at school. Some of the stories are still told today, by people who are descended from those ancient people who told them for the first time thousands of years ago. Some have changed so much that the ancient people who first told them would no longer recognize them.

Like the ancient artifacts in the book, these tales have moved around the world. The story of how they moved is also a story of migration, colonization, war, trade, and friendship. Unfortunately, it has been the case for far too long that certain ancient people were considered more important than others (usually those who lived in what is now called Europe). As a result of this, some stories are better known than others. I hope that in this book you will meet gods and goddesses that you haven't met before, and become inspired by them to learn more about the whole of the ancient world.

None of the stories in this book belong to me. Some of these stories came to me from people who told them at bedtime, around campfires, or while eating their dinner—people who are descended from the ones who told these stories for the first time. I read others in books. Some of these books were written by Europeans, who learned the stories from people they colonized. They often deliberately misrepresented the myths and beliefs of ancient people, in order to make other cultures seem less successful and less complex than their own. In retelling these stories, I have tried to unravel the untruths that colonizers had woven into them.

The history of these stories is complicated and often painful. But telling them has never been more important. Each of the gods and goddesses in this book is proof of ancient humans trying to make sense of stars, or storms, or hunger, or grief, or love. Hidden in the courage of heroes or the cleverness of princesses, knotted through mysterious spells and cunning tricks is the proof that humans have always needed to rely on each other as much as they have ever needed to rely on gods. Myths show us how much we need each other. They need to be told in order to stay alive. And it is up to all of us to tell them.

MAP OF WORLD MYTHOLOGY

All cultures started small, as groups of people who came together to survive. Over time, they developed ways of living and shared beliefs, began to make art and tell stories. The stories in this book come from ancient cultures around the world. Some people lived in what we would now call countries. Other groups of people shared a language or a religion. This map shows where the stories originated, but each tale has now traveled the world, changing and passing from person to person until it was written down in this book.

Hawai'i

Wabanaki
(Indigenous
American)

Maya

Taíno

Tahiti

Norse
(Scandinavia)

Slavic

Ancient
Greece

Mesopotamia

Hinduism

Buddhism

Japan

Akan

Ancient Egypt

Zoroastrianism

Vietnam

Yoruba

Central and
Southern Africa

N

W   E

S

Aotearoa

HOW THE WORLD BEGAN

Was there a time before the world began? For the people who have lived in Australia since ancient times, the era before time began was called "Everywhen," while the ancient Greeks called it "Chaos." Some of the stories that ancient people told about how the world came to be might seem far-fetched. But even today we are still wondering whether anything came before the Big Bang. It is not surprising then that ancient people came up with so many different ideas for how the world began.

THE HEART OF PTAH

The ancient Egyptians had many different ideas about who—
or what—had created the world. But all of the theories began with
the sea. The dark watery depths of the sea were all that there
was. It is impossible to say when, because time had not yet begun,
but one day the Sun was born. The Egyptians called this day
"The First Moment."

Some believed that a huge blue lotus flower had floated across
the ocean and unfurled its petals to reveal a baby who cast bright
rays out over the whole world. They named the child Atum—the
Sun and also the creator of the world.

Atum was neither male nor female, and had one extremely
powerful all-seeing eye. They had been living all alone at the
bottom of the sea before time began. Using this loneliness as
building blocks, Atum made Shu, the god of air, and Tefnut,
the goddess of moisture. Shu and Tefnut grew in Atum's mouth
and when they were ready to be born, Atum spat them out into
the world.

There was another story that said that Shu and Tefnut had been born under even more mysterious circumstances. The sea in which the world began had a name: Ptah. There were no humans yet to see Ptah, but if there had been, they would have seen a man, much smaller than most, with green skin, a long beard, and legs that pointed in opposite directions.

Ptah could do extraordinary things. He could bring the whole world into existence by willing it with his heart and speaking it out loud. And so Ptah—some believed—spoke the names of Shu and Tefnut, and they existed. Then he spoke the names of eight other gods, and they existed, too.

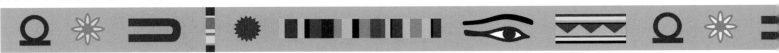

The eight gods helped Ptah to organize the universe. They were paired together and each pair represented one of fluidity, darkness, the infinite, and rest. Shu and Tefnut went on to have two children, Geb and Nut. Geb was the god of the Earth, whose laughter created earthquakes and who was known as the father of the snakes. Nut was the goddess of the stars in the night sky, and carried a ladder with her wherever she went so that she could go up into the sky whenever she needed to. Nut and Geb were the parents of Osiris, Isis, Set, and Nephthys, and it is from them that all of the other Egyptian gods descended.

Humans were an afterthought for both Ptah and Atum. In fact, the existence of humans was entirely accidental. Many centuries passed and the world thrived in perfect harmony without any humans at all. But as Shu and Tefnut grew older—many centuries older, though they didn't look different since gods age much less quickly than humans—they began to be curious about the depths of the ocean that surrounded them.

Shu and Tefnut went off one day to explore the ocean and never returned. They disappeared into its darkness, and although Atum searched throughout the watery world for them, they could not be found anywhere. Eventually, Atum sent their one eye throughout the whole world to look for the pair. Desperately sad to have lost their only children, Atum began to cry. From each one of the tears Atum cried, a human sprouted. Eventually, the eye found Shu and

Tefnut, and Atum was so happy that they cried all over again—only this time it was gods and goddesses that came from each teardrop, not humans.

Although the humans had come into existence by accident, they never stopped thanking the gods and goddesses for the gift of life. They prayed exactly as Ptah told them to, and they built enormous temples to worship the deities who had made the world and put them in it. The Egyptians had a special relationship with the sun god, who they called by different names—Atum, the Sun who gave life to everything, Ra, the god of the midday brightness, and Horus, the god of its setting and rising.

The Egyptians imagined that the Sun was carried on a ship across the ocean. Just as the sun rises from the ocean in the morning and sinks back under it in the evening, they believed the world too had risen from the depths of the sea and would one day be returned to watery darkness again.

EGYPTIAN GODS

The ancient Egyptians loved showing their gods in sculptures, drawings, and writing. They believed art provided the spirits of gods and goddesses with a resting place on Earth—they could also rest inside people and animals, or in natural phenomena like storms or floods. Ancient Egyptian artists were more interested in capturing this spirit than with showing what the gods might actually have looked like.

Many gods in one

There were so many Egyptian deities that it is impossible to count them. People worshipped the ones who were important in their lives: sailors might worship the crocodile gods of the Nile, and pregnant women worshipped Bes, the protector of children. People also combined their favorite gods into one—this figurine has the head of a falcon, the body of a crocodile, and a disc on its head showing it is also a sun god.

Motherly love

Many Egyptian gods were not strictly male or female—some did not have a gender, or took on different ones at different times. Among the gods with genders, female ones were no less important than males. In Egyptian mythology the love of a mother is often shown to be the most important force in the universe. This image shows the goddess Isis feeding her son Horus.

God of the dead

Anubis, the god of the Underworld, was often depicted with the head of a jackal, a type of wild dog. Egyptian gods were not always good or kind, and many people worshipped them mostly because they were afraid of them. Anubis weighed the hearts of dead people to decide whether they had been good enough to enter the realm of the dead. Souls whose hearts were weighed down with bad deeds would be fed to Ammit, a monster with the head of a crocodile, the claws of a lion, and the body of a hippopotamus.

The goddess Isis was often shown with a sun disc and cow horns on her head. Osiris was shown as a mummy wearing a crown with ostrich feathers attached, holding a shepherd's crook and a whip.

The original mummy

The Egyptian gods were not immortal. They could be hurt, and even die. Osiris, the god of agriculture, was murdered by his brother Set, the god of storms and violence, who wanted to seize his power. Set chopped Osiris into pieces and sprinkled them across Egypt. Isis, Osiris's wife and goddess of magic and healing, collected the pieces of her husband's body and wrapped them up. After his death, Osiris became the ruler of the afterlife, and the way that his wife wrapped his body was said to be the origin of the famous Egyptian practice of mummification.

Blue eyes

The piercing eye of Horus was worn as an amulet for protection and to encourage healing. This bright blue amulet is made from a material called "Egyptian faience," similar to glass. Its bright color comes from a glaze made with copper, which looked like much more expensive precious stones such as turquoise or lapis lazuli.

Parting gifts

Small amulets are often found inside the wrappings around mummies. Many Egyptians were buried with images of the chosen gods they had prayed to during their lives, or one showing Nephthys (right), the goddess who protects the dead. Removing these objects from the mummies is a practice that many archaeologists disagree with, because it involves disturbing burial sites and digging up the bodies of real people.

OUT OF CHAOS

For the ancient Greeks, the world began with a strange and shapeless place called "Chaos." All things were mixed in together: wet was mixed with dry, good with bad, and light with dark. There was no day and no night, and all the minutes and hours that would later make up time were jumbled together. Then, a nameless god changed all of this. He sifted the land out from the sky and squeezed the sea out of the air. He fished the stars and the Sun and Moon out of Chaos and hung them one by one in the sky. He gave everything a name and a place.

Now that the world had been put in order, it found its own rhythm. The sea flowed toward the shore and back out again, and the Sun began to find its way across the sky every day. For a while everything seemed perfect. Gods and goddesses, giants and monsters all lived peacefully together. There was no need for laws because everyone was good without even thinking about it. The Earth offered all kinds of fruits and vegetables as food. The Greeks called time "the Golden Age."

The god Kronos was the youngest child of the Earth and the sky. He lived in constant fear that one day he might have a child who became more powerful than himself. As soon as his wife Rhea gave birth to each of their children, Kronos opened his mouth wide and swallowed the baby whole. Each time, Rhea pleaded

with Kronos to forget about his obsession with power and control and to let their child live. But he refused.

By the time Rhea felt her sixth child kick inside of her, she had a plan. She went to the island of Crete where she hid in a cave and gave birth to a boy, who she called Zeus. But Kronos leaped over the sea, banged on the door of the cave, and demanded Rhea come out. Rhea asked the nymphs who lived there, who sometimes took the form of women, and sometimes of bees, to keep Zeus safe. They buzzed with fear, but promised that they would take good care of the child if Rhea convinced Kronos to leave them alone.

**Head of Zeus,
3rd or 2nd century BCE**

This head was carved from marble. Zeus is usually depicted with a beard, showing his authority as father of the gods.

Rhea was ready. She picked up an infant-sized rock from the floor of the cave and wrapped it in a blanket. She kissed the real baby Zeus goodbye, leaving him in the care of the bee-nymphs, and stepped out of the cave, cradling the rock in her arms as if it was a baby. Kronos snatched the bundle from her and swallowed it whole. Then he grabbed Rhea and went back to Mount Olympus.

When Zeus was older, the bee-nymphs told him what had happened to each of his brothers and sisters. In shock, he stormed out of the cave and stomped along the beach, trying to decide what to do next. The waves began to whisper to him. Suddenly, a woman appeared out of the sea foam, and offered him a potion that would bring his brothers and sisters back. He decided to give it a try.

Zeus tracked down his father Kronos and sneaked the potion into his drink. As soon as it touched Kronos's lips, he started to groan and clutch at his stomach in pain. He staggered three steps to the left and then three steps to the right and then vomited a huge wave, on which floated all of Zeus's brothers and sisters. Hestia, Demeter, Hera, Hades, and Poseidon were all there—along with the rock that Kronos had swallowed instead of the infant Zeus all those years ago.

The Golden Age was over. Kronos and his brothers and sisters went to war against Zeus and his brothers and sisters, until eventually Zeus's side won and ruled over all the world. All the world that is, except humans—because they had not been created yet. Zeus gave the task of creating humans to the giant Prometheus. His brother Epimetheus was tasked with giving the gifts of the gods to all of the Earth's creatures. Prometheus spent several days selecting the best material, and eventually chose mud, which he carefully sculpted into human form with his

fingers. He asked the goddess Athena to breathe life into the mud figures. Epimetheus had been working hard, too. He had given cats their curiosity, elephants their long memory, and bats their ability to find their way in the dark. But by the time Prometheus had brought the humans to life from mud, his brother had no gifts left to give.

Prometheus was disappointed that Epimetheus had not kept back any gifts for his humans. He promised them something special—that they alone would have the ability to make fire. He lit a torch from the Sun and brought it back down to Earth. Prometheus had made his humans special but at great cost— fire had belonged to the gods and when they found out, they were going to be angry. From that time on, the Greeks worshipped the gods partly out of fear of being punished for the fire that was stolen when the world was just beginning.

THE WORLD THAT CAME FROM A SHELL

Each of the Pacific islands has its own story for how the world was made. In Tahiti they said that it all began with a shell. There was no Earth, no land, no sea, and no time—just a single shell. And in that shell was a single god: Ta'aroa.

Ta'aroa had been curled up all alone in his shell for all of eternity until one day he decided to stretch his arms and legs, and step outside. He slid out carefully and stood gazing at the enormous, empty expanse of the universe. He called out across the dark nothingness, but there was no reply. He was all alone. He got back into his shell, curled himself into a ball, and stayed there for another eternity.

Eventually, he came out again. He was still alone and, although he would not have admitted it even if there had been anyone to admit it to, he was lonely. Suddenly, he had an idea. What if he and his shell could create a whole world? That way, he would never be alone again. He broke off the curved side of his shell and held it up to make the sky. Then he cupped his hands together to make the Earth and everything in it.

Father and mother

This carved wooden panel shows Ranginui and Papatūānuku with all their children around them. It was made to decorate the front of a storehouse in 18th-century Aotearoa (New Zealand).

Across the ocean on the island of Aotearoa, the ancient people told a different story. Here, people said that the sky, named Ranginui, and the Earth, named Papatūānuku, were parents to many children, who lived squeezed inside the darkness between them. There was Tūmatauenga, the god of war, Tāwhirimātea, the god of weather, and Tāne, the god of the forests and birds. There was Rongo, the god of growing food, and Haumia, the god of gathering food. There was Tangaroa, too, their name for Ta'aroa. Tangaroa was the god who created scaly creatures, like fish and lizards. But none of the children could be the gods of any of these things yet, because nothing existed except the sky father and the Earth mother and their children, and the darkness.

As the children got older, they grew tired of living in darkness. They dreamed of a different world, where there would be light and space to stretch out their limbs. In whispers, so that their parents would not hear, they planned their escape. Tūmatauenga spoke first. He was angry that his parents had kept them cooped up in the dark all this time. He wanted to kill them. But the other siblings refused to do it. Tāne had another idea—they could push their parents apart and free themselves.

Rongo reached up and tried to push the sky father upward, away from the Earth mother, but their grip on each other was too tight. Then Tangaroa tried. It was as if their parents each had as many arms as an octopus, and held tightly to one another with each limb. Eventually, Tāne tried, lying on his back and pushing with both of his legs against the sky until a tiny chink of light opened up between their parents. Stars rushed in, first one by one and then thousands all at once, and Tāne stacked them up into pillars so that their father was pushed further and further up into the sky away from their mother.

The siblings blinked, wide-eyed, at a light they had never seen before. When Tāne was finished, he went up to the sky and sat with his father. As a way of making amends for having separated him from the Earth mother, he collected together all the lights that he could find and hung them in the night sky. These stars, he thought, would make a suitable outfit for his father to wear.

The other siblings set about building the rest of the world. All of them, that is, except brother Tāwhirimātea, who was angry. He had not joined in the escape plan, and was upset that the only life he had ever known had changed forever. He joined his father in the sky and started to attack the trees to punish the forest god Tāne, sending harsh winds that blew away the leaves. Then he set on Tangaroa, who fled into the ocean and became the god of the sea. Every day the sea, Tangaroa, would flee away from his brother, Tāwhirimātea, and then return. This created the tides.

Almost as soon as the sea and the land had been created, they filled up with humans—though no one could ever agree on exactly how the humans came to be. More and more humans filled up the islands, bringing love and life, and friendship and families. Very soon the humans had spread all across the world. The endless darkness did not return. And Ta'aroa would never know loneliness like the eternity he had spent all alone in his shell ever again.

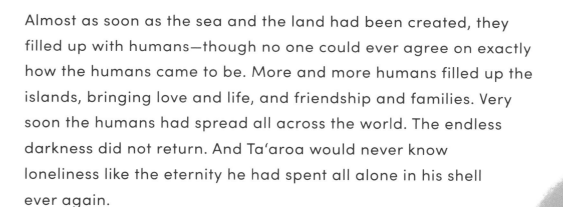

SURVIVOR GODS

The fact that we know the names and stories of so many ancient gods and goddesses today is surprising. History is full of moments that might have deleted them from our collective memory altogether. Empires often attempted to control which gods were worshipped by the people they conquered. This was as much the case in the ancient world as in the colonial era and the modern day, when people are still persecuted for what they believe. Remarkably, even as their altars, their religious objects, and even the worshipper themselves were destroyed, belief in many of these ancient gods survived.

ZEUS / JESUS

Old gods made new

When the Romans changed their religion to Christianity, they did not immediately give up on their old gods. Roman statues of Jesus look so much like the Greek god Zeus (who the Romans called Jupiter) that it can be hard to tell who it is that each statue shows. This statue survived but its label did not. It either shows Jesus or Zeus, but even experts do not know which one it is!

Sharing ideas

Sometimes when religions are only practiced by a small number of people, they have to build relationships with larger groups of people in order to survive. Islam was once a very small religion. Soon after it was founded in the seventh century, it made its way to China along the Silk Road, an ancient trade route that went all the way from China to Europe. This tile tells a story of sharing and collaboration between Islamic and Chinese art. It comes from a Persian palace, but shows a Chinese mythical bird at the center. It would have been surrounded by other tiles showing Chinese dragons.

Stolen treasures

From the 15th century onward, European powers attempted to control parts of the globe, particularly the Americas, much of Africa, and Asia. Large numbers of people were enslaved, killed, and eventually colonized by these European invaders, and a lot of knowledge about the gods and goddesses they worshipped was lost. Colonizers often forced people to change their religion to Christianity. They either destroyed art that showed older gods, or stole it to take back to European museums. This statue, which shows a priest, was looted by British military forces, who destroyed the city of Benin and massacred its people.

The Yupik are skilled at using as many parts of an animal as possible, to avoid any waste. This mask is bound together with the dried intestine of an animal such as a seal, that was hunted to provide food.

A goddess returns home

This statue, of the Hindu goddess Pratyangira, is over 900 years old. It was stolen from a temple in Tamil Nadu and then sold to a museum in Australia. In recent years, many more people have begun to understand that it was wrong to steal these precious objects from where they belonged. This statue of Pratyangira was returned to where it had been taken from—and around the world many other objects are being returned from museums to their homes as well.

Gateway to the spirit world

This mask was made by Indigenous Yupik people from Western Alaska in the 1800s, but it illustrates beliefs that are much older. The Yupik people believe that all living things have a spirit, and that the line that divides the human world from the spirit world is not always clear. In this object, the four circle-shaped holes represent a passage between different worlds. When Russian and European missionaries arrived in Alaska, they tried to convert many of the Yupik people to Christianity, but some of their older beliefs survived.

THE CHAMELEON
AND THE LIZARD

The people of ancient central and southern Africa had many names for the mysterious god who created the world—Nyambe, or Mulungu or Unkulunkulu, and many other names besides—but they did not know exactly how the world had been created. They did know that this god was very powerful, but could also be kind and generous.

For a long time the sky had hung low over the Earth, but there came a time when Mulungu—to use one of the god's names—moved away, pulling the sky up with him. In every town there were whispers of what they had done to upset their god. Was it the cooks who had angered him, beating their pestles too loudly while grinding up herbs and spices? Or did the smoke from the fires that humans used to heat their homes itch the god's nose? Some claimed it made the god cry to see animals hunted and killed for food.

Occasionally someone would climb up to the sky and try to find out, but gods speak in riddles and no one ever came back with

a clear answer. Mulungu was not always cruel to the humans. In fact, when a woman who had lost her baby in the bubbling waters of a nearby stream climbed up into the sky to beg Mulungu to bring her child back from the dead, he granted her wish. When she returned back to Earth, the woman was clutching her baby to her chest, and no one would have known that the little girl had drowned that day in the river except for the fact that her clothes were wet.

The humans wanted to know how Mulungu had created the world—and how he had created them. Most people simply assumed that the universe had always existed, and that the animals and plants and seas and rivers had been there since the beginning of time. One man would say that his grandmother had seen a reed explode, revealing a human wrapped between its leaves—maybe that was the answer? He said the reeds were different colors, and that the skin of the human that exploded out from within their leaves matched the color of the reed.

Someone else would argue that this story was not true—her uncle had told her that humans opened up the trunk of a tree and walked straight out into the world, with cows and other farm animals following behind them. There were others who said that they had heard the story told differently, and that humans had not walked out of a tree, but out of a cave or a hole in the ground, or floated up from a lake. The first humans would sit up until late at night talking the matter over, but they could never agree.

There was one story, however, that people could agree on. However they had arrived there, once the humans were around, it was up to Mulungu to decide whether they would be immortal and live forever like him, or live and die and move on to the spirit world, like the animals. Mulungu thought long and hard about this decision, and eventually he decided that humans should live forever. He called the Chameleon to him and asked him to go to the humans and tell them that they would not die, but would live forever in the new world they had just entered. The Chameleon set off down to Earth to bring the god's message.

By now it was a long way between the sky, where Mulungu lived, and the Earth, where the humans lived. Chameleons move slowly and take their time with each of their movements, and so by the time the Chameleon reached the Earth, the number of humans had almost doubled. Mulungu was starting to have second thoughts. He looked down from his seat in the sky at the whole of the Earth below. It had seemed so vast when there were only a few humans, but now it looked smaller and smaller, and he began to wonder whether it would have enough space for all of the humans who would be born for the rest of time.

Mulungu became more and more convinced that granting immortality to the humans was not a good idea. He called the

Lizard to his seat in the sky and asked her to go down to Earth as quickly as possible and to tell the humans that they would not be immortal, and they would come to the end of their lives and die just like the rest of the animals. The Lizard's eyes lit up. Although she would not have admitted this to Mulungu, she had been a little bit jealous at the idea that the god preferred the humans to all of the other animals. She crawled off back down to the Earth.

As she was dodging through the stars in the sky, the Lizard passed the Chameleon, who was moving much more slowly. She arrived at the surface of the Earth and made her way to the homes of the humans and told them what Mulungu had decided: from now on, humans would live and die just like other animals. On that day the humans learned for the first time what death meant. But they also learned something else—that they and the animals had something very important in common and that they must never allow the bond that existed between them to be broken.

YMIR AND ODIN

In Norse mythology, before the universe began there was nothingness, divided equally into two worlds. There was the world of mist, where nothing could live because it had no land or sea and was only swirling darkness and the kind of cold that bites at your bones. There was the world of fire, where flames continued to spit and roar after there was nothing left for them to burn. In between there was a void, a place of total nothingness that opened up like a wide yawn and would later be called Ginnungagap. Where the icy mist met the flames the temperature was almost liveable, although no one lived there yet.

Sometimes the flames from the world of fire reached high enough to melt the ice in the world of mist, and poisonous drips fell into the space in between. Eventually a pool gathered in Ginnungagap. The pool was not empty. Someone was lurking in its depths— something like a human, though not a human exactly. It was Ymir, who was larger than the whole of the universe, and who was not male or female but both, neither and somewhere in between.

Ymir was not alone in the pool. They were joined by an enormous cow, who fed Ymir with her milk. The cow reached up with her enormous tongue and licked blocks of ice in the world of mist until they turned to water. The cow was called Audhumla, and as she licked the ice, a human emerged. She licked once and a human's

eyelashes, two knees, and the tips of toes appeared. Then she licked again and you could make out thighs and most of a face, and the unmistakable shape of a belly button. On her third lick, a man stepped out of the ice block and dropped down into Ginnungagap. The man was Buri, the grandfather of all the gods.

Ymir had missed all of this happening, because they had been asleep, their cosmic snoring shaking all of the universe. While they slept, Ymir gave birth—by accident, from under their armpits— to a small family of giants. These were the giants from which every giant who came after was descended. One of these giants fell in love with Buri and together they had a son, who in turn had three sons, named Odin, Vili, and Ve.

The three boys grew up, trapped in Ginnungagap. Outside the pool, their only options were to freeze to death in the world of mist or burn to a crisp in the world of fire. They dreamed of a world where there were other children to play with and fields to wander and lives to lead. When they played the kind of make-believe games that only children know how to play, they imagined that they were building an entire world and filling it with forests and mountains and humans and animals.

Eventually, the brothers grew old enough to make that world a reality. Since Ymir had within them all of the elements that the brothers would need to build the world, the brothers killed them first of all. From the bones they made the mountains, from the blood they made the seas and rivers and lakes, and from the teeth they made each of the stars in the sky. They were so swept up in their work that they did not even stop to consider what the giants would do when they found out someone had killed their father. Once they had finished, Odin, Vili, and Ve began to grow afraid of the giants' revenge. They plucked out each of Ymir's eyelashes and used them to build a wall around the middle of the world where they would live. They called this place Midgard.

Midgard was a beautiful but lonely place. Odin, Vili, and Ve wanted some company. At the edge of the sea they found two small pieces of driftwood lying on the shore. Odin picked them up.

Ve wanted to ask whether any of them could remember which part of Ymir's body they had been made from, but the look on Vili's face warned him that he might not like the answer. One of the pieces of wood had come from an ash tree, and the other from an elm. Odin held the two little pieces of driftwood between his fingers, and he blew on each of them, breathing straight into their wooden hearts. The little pieces of wood came to life.

Vili took the wooden pieces in his hands next, and gave them what he thought was most important for them to have—intelligence and ambition. Now that they were able to aspire to something, the pieces of wood began to wriggle about in Vili's hands. He passed them to Ve, who carved them into their shapes. He decided that one should be male and the other female. He gave them clothes made from seaweed picked up from the shore, and told them that they would have names: Ask for the man, and Embla for the woman, after the trees they had come from. Then he set them down on the beach.

Ask and Embla made a life for themselves in Midgard, safe from the giants behind the wall of Ymir's eyelashes. They built a home and raised a family. It is to that family that the Norse people believed every human could trace their ancestry. They saw their own lives as proof that the breath that Odin had breathed into the first man and the first woman had never run out.

THE WORLD THAT CAME FROM A GOURD

Deminán was the eldest son of the Taíno goddess Itiba Cahubaba, although only by a few moments—his three brothers were born right after he was. None of the boys knew anything about the circumstances of their birth at all, however, because their mother had died at that very same moment, and Deminán and his brothers had grown up all alone in the world of the spirits. Some of the other gods had been kind to them, but to tell the truth many of the gods made them feel very afraid.

One of the most frightening of them all was the supreme god Yaya. Deminán and his brothers had heard a rumor that Yaya had killed his own son because he did not want to pass his power over to him when the son became old enough to inherit the celestial realm. No one knew for sure whether this was true, but when Yaya was out of his house one day tending to the fields higher up in the spirit world, Deminán and his brothers decided to investigate. They opened the door to Yaya's house and looked around for clues. Deminán spotted a gourd hanging from the ceiling in the corner of the room.

He balanced his feet on the shoulders of his brother—who in turn balanced his feet on the shoulders of another of the brothers—so

that they were able to reach the gourd and Deminán was able to look at what was inside. Deminán looked down at his brothers in horror. He did not need to open his mouth to tell them what he had seen. The bones of a young man, not much older than the four brothers, were chopped into pieces and stowed away in this hanging gourd at Yaya's house.

One of the brothers started to feel more than a little unwell, and his legs began to shake and sway so that the tower that was holding up Deminán at the top started to become unstable. The tower of brothers toppled over and as they did, Deminán dropped the gourd that he had been holding in his hands. It fell to the floor and the hard flesh on the outside of the vegetable cracked open as it hit the ground. Out of the crack came a huge flood unlike anything Deminán or his brothers had ever seen before, even in the rainy season. It swept them off their feet and they were carried away in its rush to a place that none of them recognized.

The water created the Caribbean Sea—the sea that would surround the lands on which the humans would live, though humans did not exist yet. Each of the bones that had been hidden in the bottom of the gourd became a fish, and filled the newly created seas with life. The four brothers wandered around this new world, looking for a place to call home, until they stumbled across the house of a spirit of fire, called Bayamanaco. Bayamanaco recognized the boys immediately and told them that he was their grandfather—he explained that their mother had been the great goddess Itiba Cahubaba.

Bayamanaco invited the four brothers into his home and made them some cassava bread. The brothers were hungry, and Deminán snatched it from Bayamanaco's hands before he even had the chance to offer it. Suddenly, Bayamanaco turned on Deminán, shouting and spitting at him with all of the rage that you would expect from the spirit of fire. Deminán turned away from Bayamanaco's fiery outburst, and the spirit's saliva landed on his back.

Deminán's back began to burn as if he had fallen into a pit of flames, and it began to swell with large sores that appeared all the way up his spine. Deminán screamed and called for his brothers to do anything they could to stop this burning, and then he passed out from the pain.

None of the brothers knew what to do. They stared at each other for what seemed like an eternity—though it could only have been about half a moment—without saying anything at all. Then the youngest of the brothers grabbed a metal weapon that Bayamanaco kept by the door in case he was attacked, and broke open one of the fiery welts on Deminán's back. A turtle slipped out of the welt, and she swam out into the sea. The turtle, who was called Caguama, became the Earth on which all of the humans and animals would live. The brothers made their homes on Caguama's back, and Deminán asked his brothers to promise that they would always do what they could to protect Caguama and keep the Earth safe.

Carving, 12th century

Turtles appear in art all around the Caribbean Sea. This Taíno carving shows a bird standing on top of a turtle. Priests used it in their spiritual rituals.

THE TAÍNO PEOPLE

The Taíno people were one of the earliest people to live in the Caribbean. There is a lot that we do not know about their society and religion, because the evidence was destroyed by the Europeans who sailed to their shores to take their land and resources. The Europeans killed and enslaved many of them, and others died as a result of diseases that the Europeans brought with them. For a long time it was thought there were no living Taíno people left, but some of their descendants have survived. As well as the people and some of their objects, words from the Taíno language have also survived. Spanish invaders took the word "barbacoa" back to Europe, which became the English word "barbecue." The word "hammock," used to describe beds made from netting that are hung between trees, comes from the Taíno word "hamaca."

Carved shell

Like all ancient people, the Taíno used materials they found in the natural world around them. As they lived by the Caribbean Sea, they used seashells to make art. This conch shell has been carved with designs, including a skull, which was an important symbol to the Taíno people.

Ancestors

Taíno people carved images of their ancestors, called zemís. Zemí is a Taíno word that means both the object you can see and the spirit that might come and inhabit it. Taíno people believed that everything in the natural world had a spirit. Trees, animals, storms, artworks, bones, and even people could all be inhabited by the gods. Some zemís were small and could be worn as jewelry, like this one, and others were big and used in religious ceremonies and rituals. They were usually made from wood, stone, bone, or shell.

Seat of power

As well as shell and ceramic, Taíno artists were also experts at carving things out of wood—like this chair. These special seats were called duhos and were used by chiefs and other important people during rituals. They usually have the head of a god or an ancestor carved onto them. Duhos are low to the ground so that the person could lie almost flat during the ritual.

In this stone representing the cassava plant, you can see that the artist has carved a face to bring the spirit of the cassava to life. Can you spot an eye and a mouth?

Strong women

Women had power in ancient Taíno society. They were leaders and could even become chiefs of the villages where they lived. At religious ceremonies, women would offer the zemís a special bread made out of the root of the cassava plant ground into flour. When the Europeans arrived in the Caribbean, they were shocked to find that the Taíno women had so much power. They kidnapped them and forced them to marry European men, to try to restrict their freedoms.

LORD OF THE DANCE

The Hindu gods Brahma, Vishnu, and Shiva form the supreme trinity. They all have a part to play in the creation of the universe, which has happened many times over—as the god Shiva knows best of all. In the beginning, there was only an ocean of nothingness. Floating on it was a giant serpent called Ananta Shesha Naga, which means "serpent without end." The serpent was there before time itself and would be there after it ended.

Between Ananta's coils, the god Vishnu slept. He had been the creator of the universe before and was about to become its creator again. Cutting across the world's silence, there came a single syllable: Om. The vibrations of the sound woke Vishnu gently from his sleep. The sound filled up the world, and where there had been nothing there was now something again. Time started, and the days began turning in their cycle.

Vishnu felt a familiar bubbling in his belly button and out of it sprung a lotus flower. The lotus flower unfurled its pink petals and revealed the god Brahma. Brahma looked at Vishnu with each of his four heads, like he knew what he was about to ask him to do. "I would like you," Vishnu said solemnly, "to create the universe again." And with that, Vishnu and Ananta disappeared, leaving Brahma and the lotus flower floating on an empty sea.

Brahma wasted no time in getting started. He broke one of the petals off the lotus flower and he stretched up through the air and beyond the sky and turned the petal into the heavens. Then he turned another petal into the Earth, and with a third petal he made the skies that sat between the two. Brahma did all of this calmly and slowly, and he broke off each of the petals with a rhythm that was almost musical.

The sound of Om, coupled with this rhythm, turned into celestial music. Brahma opened his mouth to sing but instead of his voice, out came the goddess Saraswati, fully formed with musical instruments and books in her hands. Saraswati was the goddess of music and knowledge. Looking around at this world that Brahma had created, she felt that it was too disorganized and messy. It was not the kind of place that humans would like to live in. She taught Brahma how to organize the universe, putting the Sun and Moon in their familiar places in the sky, and separating the land from the water so that humans could build their homes somewhere dry.

Brahma appreciated Saraswati's wisdom and asked her to marry him. She agreed, and eventually they had a son called Manu. He was not born in the ordinary way—he came straight out of his father's mind. Brahma later had other children in this way, and it is from them that all humans are descended. The humans took their name from the very first child (the Sanskrit word for humans, "manava," means "descendants of Manu").

The humans lived and died, and lived and died, and lived and died, as humans do. And as they grew in numbers and in generations, the rhythm of their lives and their deaths began to be heard by the gods. It sounded like the beat of a drum, like music. The god Shiva, lord of the dance, lifted his foot to start dancing—but the other gods and goddesses stopped him. The end of the age had not yet come.

A thousand years passed, and then another thousand, and the music that kept the rhythm of the humans living and dying and living and dying was becoming so loud that Shiva could no longer ignore it. He lifted his foot to begin his dance and this time, no one stopped him. His wife, the supreme goddess Parvati, stood up and got ready to join in. Shiva looked across at his wife with his third eye and began. He danced, at first slowly, and then quicker and quicker, and soon his feet were moving so gracefully and so quickly that flames flickered between his toes. An arch of fire surrounded first him, then all of the heavens, all of the sky and all of the Earth. But Shiva kept on dancing.

The fire raged through the world and burned everything as it went, swallowing up the entire universe in its flames. At first the humans tried to put out the fire, but all of the rivers and all of the lakes and seas in the universe did not have enough water in them to put it out. The fire grew and grew until it had burned the entire universe to nothingness—including even Shiva himself. Then, when

it had run out of gods and humans and Earth and sky and heaven to use as fuel, the fire stopped burning.

The universe was empty once again. The waves of nothingness ebbed and flowed gently like the waves of the sea. On the waves of nothingness there floated a giant serpent, Ananta, and within the coiled scales of Ananta was sleeping the god Vishnu. Vishnu did not mind that he had been burned to death by the flames of Shiva's dance. He knew that it was only through the flames of destruction that the world could be born again. He dreamed of the universe that he would soon wake to create and he wondered whether this time it would be any different.

DIVINE DANCERS AND CELESTIAL MUSIC

Dancing and music have always been an important way for humans to put on a show for our gods and goddesses. Many ancient cultures had gods and goddesses of dance and performed dances to honor them. Group dance was a fun way for people to take part in their religion. Music could be used to summon spirits, or to accompany stories and prayers. It also made prayers easier to remember!

God of fun

Xochipilli was the Aztec god of dancing, as well as other fun things like feasting, music, games, and painting. He is often worshipped with his female partner, a goddess called Xochiquetzal, and together they were the god and goddess of plants and flowers. Xochipilli had a mischievous personality and although he was a god of having fun, if he thought people went too far, he gave them an outbreak of boils.

Dancing goddess

The Shinto goddess Amenouzume no Mikoto was worshipped in Japan. A cheerful goddess, she is known for a story about when the sun goddess Amaterasu went into a cave and refused to come out. Amenouzume covered herself in moss and started dancing, making the other gods laugh. Amaterasu was so curious she came outside and restored light to the world.

Colima team

These figures were made around 2,000 years ago by artists in the Colima area of western Mexico. The ceramic statue (below) shows a musician playing a drum for dancers such as the one (right) wearing an elaborate crocodile headdress.

This marble carving was made in ancient Rome in the 2nd century, to decorate a tomb. It shows all nine muses. Terpsichore is the third muse from the right.

Muse of dance

In ancient Greece and Rome, there were nine goddesses called muses, who inspired the arts. Each one was responsible for a different type of art. The muse of dance and song was called Terpsichore. She made music for people to dance to. She was also the mother of the deadly sirens, who lived in the sea and used their beautiful singing voices to lure sailors to their deaths.

Goddess of battle

Ishtar (known in earlier history as Inanna) was an important goddess in Mesopotamia, where she was worshipped as far back as 6,000 years ago. She was the goddess of many things including music, but also of war. The act of taking up weapons and going into battle was called "the dance of Ishtar."

Dancing after death

Small pottery or wood figurines that showed entertainers in the middle of their performances were commonly buried with the bodies of dead people in ancient China. In some ancient Chinese texts, a part of the soul known as the po is thought to remain with the deceased person, so these figurines were left to comfort and entertain the po after the person's death.

GODS HELPING HUMANS

Humans have always needed help to survive in the world. In the modern world, it is technology that helps us to go beyond what humans are naturally able to do. We can communicate with each other over long distances or travel much more quickly than we could ever walk. In the ancient world, it was the gods and goddesses that humans looked to for help with these things. But in stories, the help of a god could often come at a price—gods and goddesses could be dangerous as often as they were helpful.

CHAHK OPENS UP THE MAIZE MOUNTAIN

The Maya people were so hungry that their stomachs roared instead of rumbled, and they could barely walk more than a few steps. They had searched all through their lands for something more than a small handful of berries and leaves. But they had found nothing. Each time they passed an animal that looked like it had eaten a meal that day— a monkey with a rounded stomach, or a macaw with shiny feathers, or an especially plump turtle—they would beg it to show the humans the source of its food. But the animals never agreed.

One of these animals was a gray fox, which made a point of stopping and licking her lips whenever she came across a group of hungry humans. When they asked what she had eaten, she told them about a grain called maize that had filled her up and kept her going all day. The humans would shake their heads and groan because they had never heard of this magical crop and they were sure that the gray fox must be lying to them, as she often did.

But after the sun had set, while the rest of the Maya were trying their best to sleep on an empty stomach, one woman decided to follow the fox to find out whether the magical grain was real. With only the stars to light her way, she put on a cloak over her clothes, twisted her hair into a long braid to keep it out of her eyes, and headed into the darkness. It did not take her long to find the fox, which took the same route past the same rock at the same time every morning and every evening. The woman followed the fox out of town and toward the mountains. Whenever the fox stopped and looked around, the woman hid behind one of the branches of a ceiba tree.

Eventually, the fox came to the largest mountain and stopped. The woman crouched behind a boulder and watched as the fox flicked her tongue out of her mouth and back in again. She did it again and again, and the woman could see that the fox was eating something, although she could not see what it was. She stayed there until the night was at its darkest, and the fox went back home the way she had come. Then the woman slipped out from behind the boulder and walked to the bottom of the mountain. At the base of the mountain there was a small crack in the rock, and she could see two lines of ants going in and out. The ones coming out were carrying... something. But the woman did not know what it was.

Each ant carried something golden yellow, and roughly the size and shape of a human tooth. She picked one up. She was so hungry that she did not even stop to think that it might be dangerous to eat it—which luckily, it wasn't, as she discovered when she put it in her mouth and chewed it. She plucked more and more of the magical grains from the ants that were carrying them and she began—for the first time in her life—to feel full.

But as she got fuller, the woman got angry. All the animals had kept this magical grain a secret, while the humans were starving. She grabbed one of the ants and held him up. "How dare you," she said, "keep this grain to yourselves, while children starve?" The ant was terrified, and he could not even catch his breath enough to answer her question because she was squeezing the middle of his body tightly with her two fingers.

When the woman realized that the ant could not answer, she set him back on the ground, and as he was scuttling away, he called out: "The crack in the rock is far too small. There is no way even the smallest human would fit through the gap into the maize mountain." As he said this, the ant breathed a sigh of relief—he had survived his encounter with the humans on this occasion, but his body would never be the same. For the rest of time the bodies of ants would be separated in two, as if someone had squeezed them tightly in the middle with their fingers.

The woman looked at the tiny gap that the ants were easily passing through, and she had to admit that the ant was right. She called to the gods. She apologized for how cruel she had been to the ant and for the fact that she had not trusted the fox —and she begged the gods to open up the gap in the maize mountain so that the hungry humans could go inside. Chahk, the god of the rain, was the first to hear the woman's prayer. He believed that the woman really meant her apology and would be kinder to the animals in future. He decided to help the humans.

Statue, 14th or 15th century

This head of the rain god Chahk (or Tlaloc to the Aztecs) is carved from stone that formed after a volcanic eruption.

He raised one of his arms and lifted up a lightning bolt above his head. It hit the mountain's summit with a crash that was unlike anything the woman had heard before. The mountain split in half, revealing mounds of maize, and seeds for new plants at its center. The woman ran back to the town to bring the good news. She hugged the other humans and told them that none of them would need to be hungry ever again.

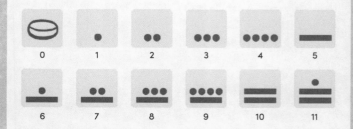

THE MAYA PEOPLE

The Maya are a people who live in southern Mexico, Guatemala, Belize, El Salvador, and western Honduras. They started building cities and ceremonial centers around 500 BCE and made many impressive advances in art, architecture, mathematics, and astronomy. Since the 1500s, when they began to be colonized by Spanish settlers, they have struggled to maintain their culture and way of life.

Calendar

The Maya used a calendar that was said to have been brought to the Maya people by the god Itzamna. The calendar was made up of three interlocking cycles. One was a 365-day solar year, similar to the year that we use to mark time today. Unlike the calendar we use today though, the Maya people split these 365 days into eighteen months of twenty days, and five remaining "unlucky" days.

Gods and goddesses

We know the names of around 250 Maya gods and goddesses. Ixchel is the goddess of medicine, and Yum Kaax is the god of wild animals. The Maya had gods to take care of the things most important to them. Many of these gods are related to farming, because the people's main source of food was what they could grow on the land. This statue (right) is the god of chocolate! You can see a cocoa pod attached to his belt.

Numbers and Writing

The Maya system of numbers is based on very simple symbols, but could be used to calculate large numbers very accurately. The ancient Maya only used three symbols to make up all of the numbers: a dot which represented 1, a line which represented 5 and a picture of a shell that stood for zero.

0	1	2	3	4	5
6	7	8	9	10	11

54

Divine kings

Maya territory was often fought over by rulers who called themselves "divine" or godlike. In this image, the king is sitting on a throne. He is wearing a feathered headdress, which shows he was rich and powerful. The Maya loved feathers so much they had a feathered god, called Kukulcán.

This carving is made of jadeite, a valuable gemstone. Its color symbolized nature to the Maya people. They put beads made of jade into the mouths of people who died.

Maya queen

The woman in this object is probably royal—we can tell this by looking at the big necklace around her neck and her elaborate headband. The inside of this carved statuette is hollow and filled with ceramic balls so it could be played as a musical instrument, like a rattle.

Incense

Maya people burned incense during their religious ceremonies and rituals. This object—called an "incensario"—was used to produce billowing clouds of smoke.

Pyramids

The Maya people built huge pyramid structures, like those of the ancient Egyptians, but with a flat top. Many different ancient South American cultures built impressive temples. The Colima people of ancient Mexico left models of their temples behind so we can get a sense of what they looked like before they crumbled due to time, weather, and destruction by invaders. This model is 2,000 years old!

ENKI AND ATRAHASIS SAVE THE WORLD

The humans were being far too loud and Enlil, the king of the gods, was annoyed. At night he struggled to sleep, and during the day he had a headache that felt like bolts of lightning hitting the inside of his skull. What annoyed Enlil most was that this was his own family's fault. The gods had created humans because they were tired of working the land themselves. They had even given them the ability to speak. As he tossed and turned in his bed, Enlil regretted this very much.

When he did manage to get a few minutes' sleep, he imagined a world of silence where there were no humans at all, just like the beginning of time before they were created. He wondered if it would be better to get rid of the humans altogether. Enlil called his brother Enki. Enki was the god of fresh waters and lived in a place called Abzu, a freshwater ocean far below the ground. Enki had always liked the humans. Enlil suspected that part of the reason Enki liked the humans so much was that the sea muffled the noise that they made.

When Enki arrived, he called to his brother in greeting. "Please don't shout like that," Enlil said. "The humans kept me awake all night." Enki was about to say that he found it so interesting that the humans made so many different noises and he had noted down their words and the sound of their hands clapping together when they danced... but then Enlil continued. "We should never have created them in the first place, Enki. Help me destroy them."

For a moment, Enki was silent. Destroy the humans? He could not imagine it. It had been his idea for the mother goddess to mold them out of clay, rolling out their arms and legs between her fingers. But Enlil continued. "You are the god of water, Enki. I want to send a huge flood across the world." Enki gulped. As calmly as he could, he explained that he would not help.

Enlil turned on Enki: "So you choose the humans over your own brother. I will flood the Earth myself—I don't need you!" There was a huge clap of thunder and then all fell quiet. Enki felt sorry for his brother, but he could not agree to killing. Enlil asked him to promise that he would not tell any of the humans about his plan, and Enki reluctantly agreed.

Now it was Enki who could not sleep. He got out of bed and went back to the Earth, straight to the house of Atrahasis. He was the wisest of the humans and lived in a house made of reeds. Enki felt a few drops of rain as he walked toward the reed house. He felt sure that Enlil's flood was coming. Enki suddenly had an idea. He had promised his brother that he would not tell the humans about the flood. But Enlil hadn't said anything about telling his secret plan to animals, or trees, or... reeds.

Enki cleared his throat and spoke: "Reeds that make up the walls of this house, listen to me!" Enki felt a little ridiculous starting a conversation with walls, but he continued. "I have something very important to tell you." Within the reed walls, Atrahasis listened. "A huge flood is coming," Enki explained, "to kill all of the humans and animals on the Earth. You need to be knocked down, reed walls, and rebuilt into a ship. And the people who live within your walls need to bring with them a pair of as many animals as they can find. This is the only way that they will survive the flood."

The reed walls said nothing in response, but inside the house, Atrahasis started gathering together the tools that he would need

to build the ship. The rain was falling harder. Atrahasis and his wife Eanna built the ship together, and when it was finished, they loaded as many animals as they could find, and waited. The water rose and rose. They breathed a sigh of relief as the ship started to float.

Meanwhile in Nippur, the gods and goddesses were upset. When she realized what was going to happen to the humans, the mother goddess started to cry. Enlil realized he had made a huge mistake. He called off the rain and eventually the water flowed away into the rivers—but it was too late for most of the humans. The goddess Ishtar was convinced that all of the humans had drowned when suddenly she saw, over the horizon, a boat made out of reeds with two tiny humans standing on its deck. Rather than destroying all humans, the gods and goddesses agreed that from now on they would control the number of people in other ways—the humans would die one by one and not all at once. This, they hoped, would ensure that there would never be so many humans, making so much noise, on the Earth again. And Enlil promised that this would be the last time he would ever plot against these fascinating creatures.

Clay tablet, c. 7th century BCE

This tablet tells the part of the story of the great flood where the humans are being too noisy. It is written in cuneiform, the world's first written language. The words were made by pressing wedge shapes into soft clay.

BETWEEN THE RIVERS

The word "Mesopotamia" means "between the rivers." It describes the region between the Euphrates and the Tigris rivers, which flow from the mountains in what is now eastern Turkey through Syria and Iraq. Between the two rivers is an area of land where it is very easy to grow food to eat, which led to ancient people making their homes there. People have been farming there for around 12,000 years! Small farming villages grew into towns and cities with fabulous palaces and enormous libraries, home to kings and queens, authors and artists, as well as to farmers.

Gods in nature

Gods and goddesses in ancient Mesopotamia appeared to humans as part of the natural world. A storm, for example, was not just caused by the god Adad, but was the god Adad himself in the sky. This man is saying a prayer to the gods. His eyes are wide open, perhaps because he is seeing a god or goddess appear in front of him as a star or the rain or some other aspect of the natural world.

Writing

The world's first form of writing was developed in Mesopotamia at the end of the fourth millennium BCE. People used a pen made from a reed and pressed it into a clay tablet, leaving straight marks. These marks became a form of writing called cuneiform. This tablet shows an exercise given to a student. They had to copy out the name of the god Urash until they could write it correctly. The tablet has widely spaced lines for a child to practice making their marks. One such tablet has been found with a bite mark made by a frustrated student!

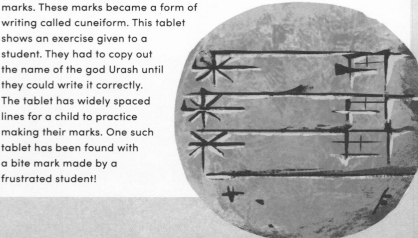

Animal forms

The walls of the ancient city of Babylon were decorated with animals, in the hope that the gods and goddesses that liked those animals would protect the city. This lion is the companion of Ishtar, the goddess of love and war. It decorates the gateway to the city alongside dragons and bulls, who are the companions of other Mesopotamian gods. You can still see some parts of the walls of the city of Babylon in Iraq today.

Answering prayers

The lama goddess, a protective goddess, had a special role in Mesopotamian religion. When humans prayed to the gods, their prayers did not go to the gods directly. It was the lama goddess who listened to the humans, and then presented their requests to the other gods. The lama goddess is usually shown holding her hands up to the gods, asking them to answer the prayers of humans.

Protective creature

Many buildings in ancient Mesopotamia had a creature called a lamassu sculpted into them for protection. A lamassu has the head of a human, the body of a lion or a bull, and sometimes the wings of a bird. If you count the number of legs, you will see that the artist has added a fifth leg to the lion part of the creature so it doesn't look like it is missing a leg when looked at from the side.

61

THE SIMORGH RESCUES ZAAL

From the moment Zaal was born, he was made to feel different to everyone else. His father Saam noticed it first—the baby's hair and skin were lighter in color than any child's he had seen before. He was convinced that the evil spirit Ahriman had made baby Zaal look this way and decided that the baby must be taken to the top of the Alborz mountain and left to die. The visitors who came to see the baby in his first days tried to tell Saam that he was wrong, he would not change his mind. There was no such thing, they said, as the evil spirit Ahriman—but Saam did not listen. He wrapped up the baby, took him to the very top of the mountain, and left him there alone.

The top of the mountain was a strange place. It was cold, so cold that Saam could feel the baby shiver in his arms when he placed him down on the ground. The ground had frozen over and glinted like a jewel. With each step the ground seemed to change color. Sometimes it looked green, then pink, then blue. Saam tried not to look into the baby's eyes because he did not want to see him cry as he walked away. Zaal wailed for what seemed like days—first because he was cold, then because his father had left him all alone, and then because he was beginning to get hungry.

All of a sudden the light was blocked out from the sky and the whole of the mountain went dark. Zaal was not alone at the top of the mountain—and this made him cry even more. The Simorgh, a huge bird whose red-gold wings blocked out the sun when she opened them, had made her home on this mountain. The Simorgh was famous throughout the world, and if Zaal had been a little older he would have known about her from stories his parents told him—but no one had told Zaal any stories. The Simorgh approached the tiny bundle, curious to see what creature was making so much noise. She pulled back the blankets that Saam had wrapped Zaal in. Two bright blue eyes stared up at her—it was a human baby. The Simorgh looked at Zaal, and Zaal stared back, trying to take in this enormous bird with red and gold feathers that looked like they were on fire when she moved. Zaal was afraid so he did the only thing he knew how to do—he started to cry again.

If you had heard the stories told about the Simorgh, you would have thought she was a bloodthirsty monster, who would open up her beak and swallow the baby whole. But instead, she picked him up between two of her giant talons and took him to her nest to keep warm. Zaal stayed with the Simorgh for years, until he was tall enough to see out over the side of the huge nest. One day some market sellers were passing in a caravan on their way back from selling their wares—business had been good and they had decided to take the scenic route home. When they returned to the city, they told everyone they knew that they had seen the face of a young man peering out of the Simorgh's nest. The news eventually reached Zaal's father Saam.

As quickly as he could, Saam climbed up the Alborz mountain. He walked past the lonely mountaintop and went even further on. Eventually he came to the Simorgh's enormous nest. Peering out over the side was a young man, with blue eyes and bright white hair the color of snow. Saam recognized Zaal instantly. Suddenly, regret hit him. This was his son, the one he had walked away from all those years ago and who would have died if this monstrous bird had not saved him. Saam dropped to his knees and prayed to his god to forgive him. He said that he was wrong to have thought that his son's bright hair and snowy white skin was a sign of an evil spirit. He was wrong to have thought his son's appearance was a sign of anything at all. And he asked his god to give him another chance to be a father to his son.

At that exact moment, the sky went dark. The Simorgh had blocked out the sun with her wings. She landed on the edge of her nest and grabbed the boy between two of her talons (Zaal was much bigger now than he had been the first time the Simorgh had carried him, but he still looked the size of a mouse in the giant bird's grip). Silently, without judging Saam for what he had done in the past, the Simorgh returned the boy to his father. She turned her head and plucked one of the red and gold feathers from her wings and let it drift down to Zaal. Then she spoke to the boy—which surprised Saam, who did not know that she could speak. "Keep this feather with you always, Zaal. If you are ever in any trouble and you need me, burn it and I will be there. Let it always remind you that when you were cold and helpless and hungry there was someone who loved you. And never forget, Zaal, that love is about something much more important than appearance." With that, she took off again, casting them into darkness until she had disappeared into the distance.

MANY GODS OR ONE?

Most ancient religions believed in many gods. Polytheism means believing in multiple gods. In polytheistic faiths, each god or goddess often represents an aspect of human life. There are gods of the weather, gods of love, and gods of science, art, or writing. In faiths where there is only one god—known as monotheism—the god has to encompass all aspects of human life. This is a tall order even for a god! In religions that have only one god, the god is also usually kinder, more forgiving, and less frightening than some of the gods in polytheistic religions could be.

ΑΛΕΞΑΝΔΡΟΥ

Zoroastrianism

Zoroastrianism is a very old religion—it was first recorded in the 15th century BCE. It is unusual among ancient religions because its followers only worship one god, called Ahura Mazda. The texts of the Zoroastrian religion are collected in a book called the Avesta. It is said that the Greek king Alexander the Great burned the Avesta when he invaded Persia and only a small portion of it remains. The Greek coin above was found in ancient Iran, showing us that Alexander the Great was there and wanted to prove his power by creating money.

Swapping ideas

When people from different religions live close together, their faiths can start to blend together or they swap ideas. There is a special word to describe this: syncretism. If you look carefully at this carved head (right), from a statue of the Greek god Zeus, you can see that he has the horns of a ram. He has been fused together with the Egyptian god Amun, who was often shown as a huge ram that protected the pharaoh.

Roman religions

Ancient Rome was home to many different religions. As well as people who believed in the Roman gods, Jewish people lived in the city and worshipped a single god. Judaism has very ancient origins, and dates back more than 3,500 years. The way that the people of Rome lived alongside each other and swapped influences is shown by this broken piece of a glass bowl (left). This bowl was owned by Jewish people who would have said their prayers in Hebrew, but the text is written in the official Roman language, Latin.

"Gold glass" was a luxurious material used in ancient Rome. It is made using two separate glass pieces. A design made from gold leaf is placed between them, and the two pieces of glass are melted together.

One god

Newer religions like Islam (founded in the seventh century) usually focus on one god. But before Islam arrived in Arabia, the people there worshipped lots of different gods and goddesses. People kept statues in their homes and temples that they used to talk to the gods. In the city of Mecca in present-day Saudi Arabia, three goddesses, known as al-Lat, al-Uzza, and Manat, were particularly important. This statue shows one of them riding a camel. Many of these ancient statues were destroyed by those who wanted to replace them with newer religions, but this one survived.

Buddha

Founded in India between the 6th and 4th centuries BCE, the religion of Buddhism is based on the wisdom of a prince called Siddhartha Gautama, later known as Buddha. His followers traveled widely, carrying Buddha's teachings around the world, where they were adapted to fit people's different ways of seeing things. In China, for instance, Buddhism incorporated ideas of being separate from the world from Daoism and respect for elders and worship of ancestors from Confucianism. You can see from these examples that the way Buddha looked was also changed to suit the local culture in different places.

Thailand

Pakistan

China

India

Cambodia

MARWE IN THE LAND OF THE GHOSTS

A girl called Marwe once accidentally slipped into the land of the ghosts. Monkeys were stealing the bean pods before they were ripe enough for humans to eat, and so Marwe and her brother were sent out into the family's field to scare the monkeys away. There had been a drought that year, so it was very important not to lose any of the crop. The children stayed out there all afternoon, even though it was so dry and hot that they thought they heard the tops of their heads sizzling. When they had finally chased away even the bravest monkeys, Marwe and her brother went in search of some water.

After walking for what seemed like forever, Marwe and her brother came to a pool of crystal-clear water. Marwe knelt down by the edge of the pool and started to drink, but she leaned too far forward and fell head first into the water. Her brother watched in horror as his sister sank beneath the water. He shouted and cried and called out to his sister, but it was no good—she did not come back.

He ran all the way home to his parents and he told them what had happened. Every morning after that, Marwe's father went to the pool and called out for his daughter by name, and every evening he returned home without her.

Marwe had fallen out of the land of the living. It was like a weight pulled her down and she could not swim back up, even though she was a good swimmer. Instead, she sank further and further down into the pool until she could no longer make out her brother's face. At the bottom, there was a doorway into another world. Marwe sank through an opening, and suddenly she was not swimming any more, but walking on land. Her clothes were dry, as if she had never fallen into a pool at all.

After she had been walking for only a short while, Marwe came to a house where an old woman lived, with many small children. This woman—a goddess, it turned out, though Marwe did not know that yet—looked after those who had fallen into the land of the ghosts while they were still young. The ancient goddess opened the door to her house and invited Marwe inside. She offered her food to eat and hot tea to drink—but Marwe politely refused. She had heard that those who go to the land of the dead are never allowed to return if they eat any food while they are there. The old goddess simply nodded and took the plate away. She explained to Marwe that this was the land of the ghosts, and that here there are no chores to do. Children simply spent all of their time playing. It was light here in the land of the ghosts, though it wasn't the bright yellow light of the sun but a cold blue.

Marwe stayed in the house for a few days, but then she said to the goddess, "I would like to go home to my family." Because Marwe had not eaten any food in the land of the ghosts, she was not forced to remain there forever. The goddess decided she was going to let the girl leave, if she answered one question correctly. But she was not going to make it easy for her. The old goddess held up a sack that was so full of gold that it spilled out onto the floor. In the other hand she held a small bucket of ice-cold water. "Which of these," she asked, "would you rather have? All of the gold you could ever wish for, or this small bucket of cold water to take back to your family?" There was a catch to the old goddess's question—if Marwe chose the gold, she would have to stay in the land of the dead forever.

Marwe thought back to the face of her brother staring down at her through the surface of the water as she sank into the land of the ghosts. She remembered how thirsty they had been that day when they had chased the monkeys out of the bean fields. She told the old goddess that she would prefer the bucket of cold water to all of the gold in the world. The old goddess was impressed, but she was not surprised—she could tell by her answer that Marwe was ready to leave the land of the dead.

The goddess nodded, as if to say that Marwe had given the right answer. Then she led Marwe around to the back of the house where a bucket stood full of cold water. She told the girl to dip her arms into it. When Marwe pulled them out again her wrists were covered in gold bangles decorated with gemstones and fine brass chains. Then the goddess led Marwe back to the pool, opened the door, and pushed her through it. Marwe floated back up to its surface as quickly as she had sunk into its depths. She climbed out of the pool and ran home. When she told the story to her parents and her brother they could hardly believe it, and would not have done had it not been for the gold bangles. Only a goddess could have given Marwe such fine gifts. The gemstones and gold would buy plenty of food at the marketplace. They thanked the goddess who lived in the land of the ghosts for keeping them well fed that year.

GUANYIN AND THE INVENTION OF KINDNESS

Miao Shan had always been a quiet sort of person. She liked to spend long hours in her room, thinking about the world and everything in it. But her father the king, who believed in being a harsh ruler, had other plans. He wanted her to marry as soon as possible, and so he had summoned all of the richest princes in the land to his palace to meet her. But Miao Shan did not want to marry. She wanted to be able to wake up early every morning in a quiet room, and to sit and meditate for hours on end—and she did not want anyone around to disturb her.

When the day came for Miao Shan to choose a prince to marry, she was nowhere to be found. The king raced through the palace, screaming and shouting. Not far from the palace, there was a deep forest. The king ordered his soldiers to search its depths. When they finally found her, the soldiers could not believe their eyes. Miao Shan was sitting under a tree with wild animals curled up asleep on her lap. She was so still that at first they could not even tell that she was breathing. There was a light radiating out of her that lit up the forest. As the soldiers approached, a tiger that was sleeping with his head on Miao Shan's knee woke up and growled at the men. Miao Shan patted the tiger gently and gestured for the animals to let the soldiers take her away.

By the time the soldiers arrived back at the palace with Miao Shan, the princes had all gone home. The king exploded with rage. "You know our land needs a new king. Soon I will be too old to rule with an iron fist the way I used to. Your marriage is our only hope," he snarled. Miao Shan tried to explain that strict laws and cruel punishments were not the only way to rule. She wanted to follow a different path, and to improve the lives of the people. Once everyone felt safe and had enough to eat she was sure they would no longer fight or steal from each other and would not need to be punished.

"Please, father," she said, "let me live among the religious people who work to make the world a better place. A life of giving food to the hungry will suit me much better than being a queen." The king secretly worried what would happen if he did not agree. The soldiers had told him about the strange light and the tiger. What if his daughter had magical powers and used them against him? Through gritted teeth he agreed that Miao Shan could go and live at the temple. But he sent word to the monks that she must only be given the most difficult jobs to do, threatening that if they disobeyed, he would burn their temple to the ground.

When Miao Shan arrived at the temple, the eldest monk led her out into a field where the soil was full of stones and where nothing had grown for centuries. He handed her some tools and told her to set to work growing food. Miao Shan gathered her hair into a knot on top of her head and as she did, she said a prayer. She promised the gods that if they allowed fruits and vegetables to grow in this field she would give all of them away so that the people of her father's kingdom would never be hungry again. As she lifted a heavy metal tool to dig into the soil, a huge golden dragon appeared in the air. With its tail, the dragon drew a line in the soil, and where the line had been drawn fresh water appeared. The water flowed over the whole field and all of the dried-up seeds began to sprout from the ground.

Miao Shan worked in the field night and day, until it was full of rice, and fruits and vegetables of all kinds. When the crops were ripe, she shared them out among the people, starting with those whose bellies were rumbling the loudest. Years passed, and as the people of the kingdom grew healthier and happier, the king's health

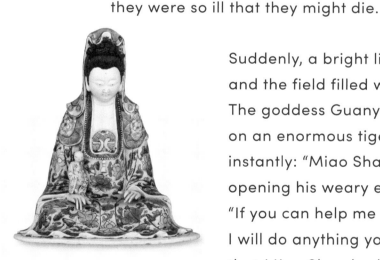

started to get worse and worse. Eventually, when the king was very sick and the soldiers could think of nothing else to do, they carried him out into the fields and prayed to the goddess Guanyin. They had heard stories about this goddess curing people with plants, even when they were so ill that they might die.

Porcelain statuette, 17th century

People kept statues of Guanyin at home to remind them to be kind and compassionate. This statue shows Guanyin with a child. She is wearing rich robes decorated with lotus and plum flowers.

Suddenly, a bright light appeared over the horizon, and the field filled with flowers of every color. The goddess Guanyin had come in person, riding on an enormous tiger. The king recognized her instantly: "Miao Shan, is that you?" he asked, opening his weary eyes to look at his daughter. "If you can help me recover from this sickness, I will do anything you ask." Guanyin—the goddess that Miao Shan had become—said that she would help the king. She asked for only one thing in return: that he would leave behind his cruelty and rule the land with kindness instead. The king readily agreed, and immediately he felt a little better. The people of his land never knew cruelty again.

TABULECH TRICKS THE CHIEF

Tabulech lived with his mother in a little wooden house next to a fast-flowing river. Although they rarely went hungry—catching just enough fish in the river each morning to feed them for a day— there was nothing left over. So when the chief of the village announced that he was taking a tax of three wampums, Tabulech and his mother were worried. A wampum was a bead made of shells that could be used to pay for things, like money. Tabulech and his mother did not even have one wampum in their little wooden house, let alone three.

Tabulech's mother brought out her most precious item, the soft skin of a moose that Tabulech's father had hunted back when he was still alive. She had tears in her eyes as she handed it to Tabulech and said, "Take this hide to the marketplace and trade it for as many wampum as you can." Tabulech hesitated, but he did as his mother asked. He set off down the road, but almost as soon as he had turned the first corner, an old man stood in his path. "What a nice moose hide you have there," the old man said, "will you give it to me?" Tabulech explained that he couldn't—he had to sell it to pay the chief's tax. "I could exchange it for this plate of food,"

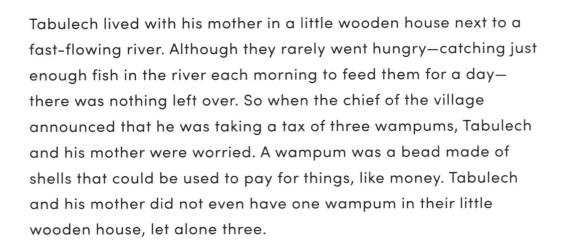

said the old man—and took from his bag a plate piled high with the most delicious meal. Tabulech felt his mouth start to water. "I can't," he repeated, "I made a promise to my mother."

The old man said that Tabulech should just try one bite. Tabulech did not want to be impolite, so he ate a mouthful—and then another and another. Before long, he felt like he was going to burst. Suddenly he realized, with horror, that he was unable to stop. It was like a curse. The old man cackled: "Give me the moose skin, and I will let you stop eating." Tabulech handed over the hide glumly, and set off to tell his mother what had happened. She had an idea who her son had met. She had heard about Gluskab, who liked nothing more than playing tricks on humans.

The next day she gave her son a fish to sell, and told him not to stop and speak to any old men. Almost as soon as he had turned the corner, a young woman stood in Tabulech's way. She wasted no time asking to trade his fish for the belt that she was holding. Tabulech said that he could not, because he had promised his mother. Suddenly, the belt slithered like a snake and wrapped itself tight around Tabulech. It squeezed until he was unable to breathe. "The belt will loosen when you give me that fish," the woman said, speaking in a low voice. Tabulech thought she sounded like the old man. He was struggling to breathe, so he did not think twice about handing over the fish. Then he returned, with the belt still wrapped around him, to his mother.

That night, Tabulech checked the traps they set to catch muskrats. Three pairs of beady black eyes peered back at him. Tabulech's mother asked him to take the three muskrats to the marketplace and to sell them for a wampum each. "And do not," his mother added, "stop to talk to any old men or young women." Tabulech set off the next day, and this time he went through a forest, where he was certain he would not meet anyone. Suddenly, he heard music. The sound of a flute grew louder, and his feet started to dance as if they had a will of their own.

He saw an elderly woman playing a flute. Tabulech danced around and around her, unable to stop his feet from moving. He placed the basket with the muskrats in it at her feet and begged her to stop playing. The old woman was laughing and she sounded just like the old man. "Gluskab!" Tabulech shouted, when his feet had stopped. "I knew it was you! You have taken everything. Now I have to go home and tell my mother that we will not be able to pay the chief. We will lose our little wooden home by the river—I'm glad you find it funny!" he added, though he was not glad at all. "Relax, young man," Gluskab—Tabulech was right, it was him—said. "You got a much better bargain than you know!" He tossed Tabulech the flute and with that, he vanished.

Tabulech returned to his mother, thinking hard. The chief was already standing outside the little wooden house. Before he could demand the three wampum, Tabulech took out Gluskab's magic

plate and set it down in front of him. The chief began to eat and could not stop even when he felt like he would burst. "I will take the plate away," Tabulech said, "if you promise not to demand any more wampum from anyone in this village." The chief agreed, but as soon as Tabulech had taken away the plate he called to his soldiers: "Kill the boy, and his mother!" Tabulech pulled out the magic belt, and it slithered like a snake, wrapping itself around the soldiers. Then he started playing the flute. The chief's feet started to dance. The chief and the soldiers danced their way out of the village and were not seen again for a very long time—and Tabulech and his mother kept their little wooden house by the river. In the end, Gluskab was right: Tabulech got a good bargain.

MOTHER GODDESSES

Across the ancient world, goddesses were celebrated for bringing new life. But for humans, pregnancy and birth was an extremely dangerous time. Many babies did not survive long after they had been born. Even when the baby did survive, life was difficult for many ancient families, who had to provide for their child without the supermarkets, cars, and medicines that we now rely on. Families turned to the gods and goddesses to ask for protection.

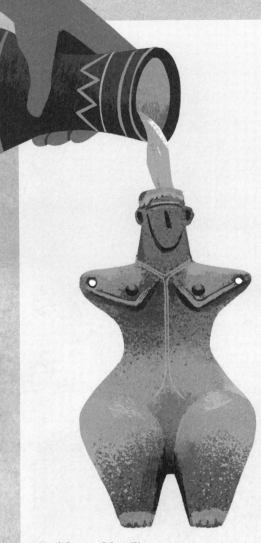

Goddess of fertility

This statue is made of clay in ancient Iran and shows a goddess of fertility. The statue is hollow, so something could be put inside it—it might have been used to present offerings to the goddess and ask her to grant fertility to those who prayed to her. In ancient Iran the goddesses of fertility were not just responsible for humans and human babies, but also for animals, fruits, and vegetables, too. Farming was an important aspect of life in this region—a good or a bad harvest could mean life or death for ancient people. Praying for the fertility of plants could also be a desperate prayer for survival.

Mother of the gods

The ancient Greek goddess Kybele was first worshipped in an area known in the ancient world as Anatolia, which now makes up most of Turkey. Kybele was brought to Greece when the Greeks colonized parts of Anatolia and were influenced by the religion of the people they met there. She was associated with lions and if you look carefully, you can spot a small lion in this statue.

Dangerous sisters

This statue shows the Hindu goddesses known as the Matrikas. They are always shown together in a group of seven or eight sister goddesses, and the elephant-headed god Ganesh has joined them here. The goddesses both cared for and threatened children. If babies or children died when they were very young, people would sometimes say that it was one of the Matrikas who had eaten them. Their statues were kept in special shrines outside of the boundaries of cities and towns, so that they could not harm the families who lived inside the city walls.

Mysterious mother

The Indus Valley people lived in the region that today is called Pakistan. We do not know very much about these ancient people because their language has not yet been deciphered, so we cannot read their myths and stories. We do know that a mother goddess figure was especially important to them, though, because hundreds of works of art like this one have been found by archaeologists in this region.

Ancestral mothers

The Dogon people have lived in Mali and Burkina Faso, West Africa, since ancient times. Some of the Dogon people believed that ancestors were like gods. Statues of mothers, who created new generations, reminded them of the importance of their ancestors. This statue shows a woman holding a very young baby. Although all babies were precious, the birth of twins was special to the Dogon people because in their creation story, the first being to be created was Nommo, a creature with the body of a fish but with legs and feet like a human. The creature split itself into four pairs of twins. These sets of twins became the first priests and leaders of the Dogon religion.

Sun goddess

Tanit was a mother goddess of the Phoenician culture, which existed in North Africa and the Mediterranean from around 1,500–300 BCE. She was the goddess of fertility but also war. Her worshippers sacrificed animals in her honor, hoping to attract her attention and get good luck from her. Tanit is usually shown as a simple figure with raised arms, as on this stela. A stela was a stone marker, often used as a gravestone.

RULERS OF NATURE

Rain, wind, the tides, and the rising and setting of the Sun were all extremely confusing to ancient people. In order to explain how these mysterious things happened, many people told stories about gods and goddesses who controlled the natural world. In some of these stories, humans praised and thanked the gods for giving them what they needed from the Earth. But the natural world could also be very frightening. Many ancient people thought that floods, plagues, fires, and storms were signs that a god or goddess was angry with them.

OLOKUN CONTROLS THE OCEAN'S WAVES

Before humans arrived on the Earth, Olokun had set it up as their own special place. It was quiet so they could concentrate on their art—making beads out of shells. Olokun was used to being asked annoying questions, especially by the other gods and goddesses. "Are you a god or a goddess?" they would ask, and Olokun would answer that they had never really felt either like a male god or a female goddess, just that they were divine. Here on Earth, Olokun did not have to deal with those kinds of questions.

The humans ruined all of that peace and quiet. As soon as they were created, they set up their homes and took up all of the space, making far too much noise. In anger, Olokun stormed off to the edge of the Earth and jumped into the sea.

84

Their legs fused together and became covered with shiny green scales. This new tail was amazingly strong. With just a little flick of the ankles, they could send a wave of water cascading over the beach. By kicking their legs a little harder, they could send an enormous tidal wave over miles and miles of the land. Olokun was a vengeful kind of god. It made Olokun laugh to watch the humans run from the waves and call to the gods for help. The humans would regret building their homes on the Earth.

The humans went to see Orunmila, the god of wisdom, and asked him what to do. He sighed and shifted in his seat—he knew what Olokun was capable of. First, Orunmila asked the god of the sky, Obatala, to send a messenger to Olokun and warn them to stop. But Olokun did not listen, and kept sending powerful waves. The humans were worried for their homes and their animals who were in danger of drowning. They went back to Orunmila. This time he told them that they should go to the home of Ogun, the god of metalwork, and ask for his help.

The humans found Ogun in his workshop, surrounded by his dogs, all of whom were sleeping peacefully. He was crafting weapons out of metal and did not hear the humans at first, over the noise of his hammer hitting the metal. The humans looked around his workshop at all of the newly forged weapons hanging on the walls, and began to worry that Ogun was going to expect the humans to fight with the powerful Olokun.

When the humans had told him about their fears, Ogun started to laugh. "Only a human would go into a battle they are certain never to win!" he said. He reassured them that he would not expect them to do any fighting. "Olokun is a powerful spirit," he said, "and deserves your respect. But they can be dangerous, as you have learned." Ogun set to work immediately crafting an enormous chain, long enough to wrap around the whole world three times. When he was finished, he told the humans his plan. "Take this chain to Obatala, the god of the sky, and he will tell you what to do." The humans lined up so that they could each carry one link of the enormous chain on their shoulders, and made their way back to the home of the sky god Obatala. The sky god already knew the plan, because Orunmila had told him— Orunmila was so wise he didn't even need to hear Ogun to know what he had said. Obatala took hold of one of the links of the chain and raised it up to the very top point of the sky. Then he positioned it over the sea where Olokun was, and let it fall into the ocean.

Pottery container, 16th–19th century

Women who wanted to have children made shrines in their homes to pray to. This water pot, decorated with a pregnant woman, was kept full of river water so that the watery god Olokun might send good luck.

The chain was heavy, so it fell through the sky and plunged into the water before Olokun could spot it. It wrapped itself around Olokun's arms and chest, and dragged them down with its weight to the very

bottom of the ocean. At first Olokun tried to fight back, but the chain had been crafted by a god and was far too strong and heavy. Olokun stayed there at the bottom of the sea for the rest of time. They never forgot how angry they were with the humans, who had not only stolen their land to make their homes but had also chained them at the bottom of the sea. By day and by night Olokun would raise their tail up and bring it down again, hoping to create another of those great waves that flooded the land and destroyed the humans' homes. But from the deepest depths of the sea, their tail fins did not have power to create more than a ripple, and so the humans lived safely on the land. And that is how the sea got its waves.

THE KINGDOM OF BENIN

The Kingdom of Benin was the ancient home of the Edo people, in West Africa (in the place that is now known as Nigeria). The kingdom—originally called Igodomigodo by the people who lived there—developed gradually from a series of small villages in a forest in the first century BCE into a huge, wealthy empire. Art made from luxurious materials such as bronze and ivory made the kingdom famous for culture as well as trade and military might.

Kings of Igodomigodo

Igodomigodo was ruled at first by a series of kings known as Ogisos, who are known to us from Edo stories. These Ogisos were later replaced by another series of rulers known as Obas. The Oba was a very important figure and to show this, Edo artists made many sculptures of them, from the metals bronze or brass.

Deep in the forest

The Kingdom of Benin started in an area of dense forest, which made the city difficult to reach and easy to defend from invaders. It provided wood and plants, and fish and other animals that the ancient Edo people could eat. Leopards were considered to be the kings of the forest, and they had a special relationship with the Obas for that reason. Artworks often show the Oba taming leopards, or fighting them—this symbolized the dominance of the Oba over the animal kingdom.

Benin Bronzes

The Benin Bronzes are famous all over the world. Sculptors from the Kingdom of Benin made thousands of them from the 13th century onward. They were hung in the palace of the Oba to remind everyone of stories from the kingdom's ancient past. This one shows a warrior chief in the center, surrounded by other soldiers. The Benin Bronzes are masterpieces of art that are now in museums around the world. Campaigners are trying to have them returned to the places they were made.

Stolen riches

Benin had skilled artists and precious materials to make objects from. Britain wanted Benin's wealth and resources for its empire. In 1897, British officials tried to force the Oba to give up control of the kingdom. The Oba's warriors successfully defended their city, but eight days later, the British returned with an army. The British Army destroyed the city, burned the palace, and stole many of the Benin Bronzes. Today, only about 50 of these works remain in Nigeria, while there are almost 2,500 in European and North American museums.

Trade with Portugal

This brass statue shows a rider wearing a crown decorated with parrot feathers. He is also wearing a European-style ruff around his neck. Portuguese merchants were the first Europeans to trade with the Kingdom of Benin, from 1489. They took leopard skins, artworks, and enslaved people back to Europe. From this time, European traders began to be represented in works of art in Benin.

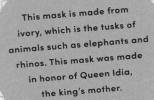

This mask is made from ivory, which is the tusks of animals such as elephants and rhinos. This mask was made in honor of Queen Idia, the king's mother.

ZORYA AND
THE SNAKE GOD

Zorya only had one job to do—but it was really important that she do it well. Every morning she would wake early while it was still dark and open the gates to the house of the Sun. And every evening when the Sun had returned home for the night, her sister would close them again. To the side of the gate every morning there lay a huge sleeping dog called Simargl, who had wings like those of an enormous bird on each side of his shoulder blades. Every morning, Zorya tiptoed past the dog very quietly and checked that his leash was still attached firmly to the Polaris star. No one knew why Simargl had to spend his life tied up like this, but everyone had heard the rumor that if he was let loose, he would gobble up the whole world, so Zorya thought it was better to be safe than sorry.

Zorya and her sister—and her father Dazbog, who by the way was also the Sun—lived on an island in the middle of a great ocean. They shared the island with the weather god Perun, who sent rain and storms and winds out from the island all across the world. At the center of the island was a huge tree, which had roots so long that they stretched down into the watery land of the dead and a trunk so high that its branches scratched at the top edge of the world. Every morning when Zorya awoke, she saw Perun

climbing up to the highest branches of the tree to look out over the whole world. From his perch he decided what the weather should be in each place on that day.

One morning when Zorya woke up and stumbled out in the dark to open the gates, something was different. Perun was not sitting at the top of the enormous tree. In fact, Zorya could not see the tree trunk at all, because coiled tightly around it was an enormous snake. Zorya recognized the snake instantly: it was Veles, god of the waters of the dead that flowed in the space underneath the Earth. Even when he was on dry land, Veles dripped water from each of his scales, and never seemed to completely dry out. But Veles never usually left the waters underneath the Earth.

There was a flash and Zorya saw Perun running toward the snake, hurling lightning bolts. Each time a lightning bolt hit the snake's body, drops of water would pour out like heavy rain. It was as if all of a sudden the stormy season had arrived. But Veles did not loosen his grip on the trunk of the enormous tree. Zorya could see in the distance that Simargl the dog had woken and was pulling at his chain as if the end of the world was near.

Perun called out to Zorya, "Open the gates quickly, daughter of Dazbog, and tell your father to drive his horses out of them as fast as he can. Veles is climbing up the tree of life and when he reaches the top, he will have control over the weather—he will make it rain for the rest of time." By the time Zorya had reached the gates and tightened the rope that kept Simargl tied to the Polaris star, Veles was approaching the highest branches of the tree. He was so much bigger and heavier than Perun that the top of the tree was starting to lean over with his weight and to swing from side to side.

Zorya swung open the gates and called to her father, who had been woken up by the commotion outside. He had already let his horses out of their stables so that as soon as Zorya opened the gate he could jump up, put one foot on each of their backs, and ride out into the night sky. In his hands he held a ball of fire. He exploded out of the gates. The sky turned from dark blue to a lighter green color and then to the pink and orange of dawn breaking. Dazbog was riding as fast as he could through the dawn sky and holding the fiery Sun above his head in one hand, and the reins of his two horses in the other. The Earth was starting to warm up.

Veles felt a sharp pain behind his eyelids—coming from the land of the dead, he was not used to the light of the Sun and its brightness hurt him. As the Sun dried out the Earth, it dried out

Veles, too, and he began to lose his grip at the top of the tree. Dazbog and his horses raced on across the sky until they reached its highest point. Veles lost his grip on the trunk of the tree of life and fell to the ground, which opened as if it had been waiting to swallow him up. There was a satisfying splash as Veles dropped back into the waters under the Earth where he belonged. Perun climbed back to the top of the tree and sent a warm breeze to dry up the watery mess that he had made in his battle with Veles. Zorya waved at her father who continued his daily journey across the sky. Simargl, who seemed to have understood that the end of the world would not come today, closed his eyes and settled back down to sleep.

THE SUN AND THE MOON

How does the Sun rise every day and set in the evening? Many of us today would still find that question difficult to answer, even with our scientific knowledge of the Earth going around the Sun. Different ancient societies answered it in different ways. Some said that a god or goddess pulled the Sun in a chariot across the sky. Others thought that the Moon was at war with the Sun about who had the right to sit at the highest point of the world. Gods and goddesses representing the Sun and the Moon were some of the most important deities in many ancient religions.

Sun charioteers

Many ancient people thought that the Sun moved across the sky because a god was carrying it in a chariot. The chariot, a small horse-drawn cart on two wheels, was one of the first vehicles ever invented. The ancient Greeks believed that the Sun rose because it was pulled across the sky by the golden chariot of the god Helios. Surya, the Hindu sun god, was carried across the sky in a chariot pulled by seven horses, which represented the seven days in a week. He was accompanied by two goddesses of the dawn, who carried arrows to fight against the darkness.

Helios

Goddess of the Moon

Artemis was the ancient Greek goddess of the Moon. She was also the goddess of wild animals and had a special relationship with bears. In one story, a baby girl called Atalanta was abandoned by her father, who had wanted her to be a boy. Artemis sent a bear, who had recently lost her cubs, to rescue Atalanta and raise her as her own cub. When she was older, Atalanta started wearing short tunics, living in the mountains and hunting, just like Artemis. In the ancient Greek city of Athens, young girls were sent to the temple of Artemis for one year just before they started puberty. While they were there, the girls were referred to as "arktoi," which means "bears" in ancient Greek.

Four directions

It wasn't just the Sun and the Moon that were thought to be controlled by gods and goddesses. While Buddhists often worshipped Surya as their sun god, they also had gods for the four directions on the map—North, South, East, and West. These were referred to as the Four Heavenly Kings. Jikokuten (left) was the god of the East, and also of music. The Four Heavenly Kings were believed to come down to Earth on specific days to check whether humans were behaving. They could be fierce when they found that this was not the case, as Jikokuten's expression shows!

Calendar

The Aztecs believed that the world was created and destroyed in a cycle, with each cycle called a sun. When this sun stone (below) was made, they thought there had been four previous suns, shown by four squares around the head of a god in the center. The Aztecs, whose empire survived until 1521, called themselves the "people of the sun" and believed they had to feed it with sacrifices of blood. The sun stone is made of volcanic stone but was originally painted in bright colors.

Sun sailors

Amun was one of the most important gods in ancient Egypt. One story tells of how he fused with the Sun god Ra into the king of the gods. Ra traveled across the world in a burning boat every day, and this is how the Egyptians explained the Sun moving across the sky. At night the Sun was not visible in the human world because the boat was passing through the land of the dead. When Ra fused together with Amun, sailing this boat became the new god Amun-Ra's responsibility. This statue is made from solid gold, a material that the Egyptians thought looked like the Sun because of its warm gleam. They even thought their gods had skin made of gold.

HOORI'S GEMS OF THE SEA

Hoori had not always lived under the sea. Back when he lived on land, he and his brother Hoderi took it in turns to go out into the shallows in a little fishing boat, to catch fish and crabs and other small things to eat. On one occasion, Hoori borrowed his brother's fishing hook and returned home having lost it in the waves. Losing a fishing hook might not seem like the end of the world to you or me, but fish from the sea was all that Hoori and Hoderi could find to eat for miles around, and so losing this hook meant several hungry days and nights.

"How could you be so careless?" Hoderi shouted at his brother. Hoori was not sure that Hoderi would ever forgive him if he did not find the hook. Even though it was nearly dark, Hoori took the little fishing boat back out to the place where he thought the hook had fallen into the waves. He took off his belt and sandals and dived into the sea to search for it. The sea was colder than he had expected, and as he swam further and further down into its depths, it got darker and darker. With every stroke of his arms he thought he saw a shark or a crocodile out of the corner of his eye, or one of the sea monsters people were always talking about.

By the time he reached the very bottom of the sea, it was so dark that he could see almost nothing at all.

He felt around on the seabed. All of a sudden he thought he saw something move—and not the small, quick movement of a fish or a crab, but the slow movement of something much bigger. It felt as if the seabed itself was shifting. He had a strange feeling in his stomach, as if he might be in the presence of something bigger than himself. He stood up—as much as possible underwater— and saw two huge eyes staring at him from the darkness, along with a set of enormous, sharp teeth. It was Ryujin, the god of the sea. "Follow me," he said.

Ryujin moved through the water like an eel. He led Hoori to his palace, which was made of red coral and shells. He told Hoori that he could stay in the palace with him and the other sea creatures until he had found the hook. Hoori wondered how he was able to breathe underwater, but Ryujin's magic somehow made it happen. Hoori stayed in the palace for nine years, going out each day to search the depths of the sea for his brother's fishing hook. In the end it was not Hoori who found it, but Ryujin himself. He placed it on Hoori's bed as if it was nothing special at all.

Hoori could not quite believe it when he saw the fishing hook lying there—he swam down the corridor as fast as he could to the throne of the sea god. "I suppose," Ryujin said sadly, "you will now want to go back up to dry land?" The sea god was surprised at how much love he felt for this boy he had found by accident. He wanted to give Hoori a gift, so he took him to his wooden treasure chest. One green and one pink jewel glistened at the bottom. Ryujin explained that he used these to control the tides of the sea. The pink jewel brought the ocean in toward the shore, and the green one sent it back away again. "I hope that your brother will welcome you back with open arms now that you have found his precious fishing hook. But if he doesn't, pick up this pink jewel and the sea will protect you." Hoori placed both the jewels into his pockets and started to swim back up to the sea's surface.

Having not walked in nine years, Hoori was a little unsteady when he took his first steps on land. He ran to find his brother as quickly as he could on his wobbly legs. He presented Hoderi with the fishing hook he had spent all of those years trying to find, but Hoderi picked it up, threw it on the ground, and pushed it into the dust with his foot. "Do you expect me to believe that you lived for nine years under the sea, spending every day searching for my fishing hook?" he sneered. Hoori did not know what to say. He really had lived for nine years under the sea, but he could see why Hoderi did not believe him—it wasn't a very likely story, even though it was true.

Hoori pulled out the jewels that Ryujin had given him to prove to his brother it was all true. He showed him the pink one first— but almost as soon as he grasped it, a huge wave lifted itself up out of the sea and crashed into his brother, knocking him off his feet. Hoderi spluttered and gasped for breath, flailing and trying to keep his chin out of the water. "Please!" he shouted, "if you really did live in the palace of the sea god, call him now and ask him to take away this wave before I drown!" Hoori put his hand into his pocket again. This time he pulled out the green jewel. The wave fell quiet instantly, and the water ebbed away. Hoderi knew that his brother was telling the truth.

GODS AND ANIMALS

Just as we love our pet cats and dogs, people in the past had particular animals they liked to show in their art. Some of these creatures were very ordinary animals, and others were ferocious mythical beasts. Many ancient gods and goddesses had a special relationship with animals. Some of them had animal companions that were often shown with them in art— these give us a clue as to which god is being shown in mysterious ancient objects. Others could transform into animals or control them.

This statue's hands and head are made from marble and the dress is made from a stone called onyx. It was carved in ancient Rome, during the reign of the emperor Hadrian (117 to 138).

Animal mummies

The ancient Egyptian god Thoth was the god of the Moon, writing, mathematics, and everything to do with learning. Ancient Egyptian gods could appear in the form of animals. Thoth is often shown in art with the head of a baboon (a type of monkey). The ancient Egyptians made mummies of animals after they had died, and buried them at temples to honor the gods. The mummy on the left is of a baboon. All sorts of animals were turned into mummies— the mummy above is of a fish!

Wise owl

The Greek goddess Athena, called Minerva by the Romans, is almost always shown with her owl companion, like the tiny one she is holding in the statue above. Athena is the goddess of war but also of wisdom, so it is obvious why the ancient Greeks associated the wise owl with her. Coins that were used in the city of Athens, which was named after the goddess, had a picture of Athena on one side and an owl on the other.

Half snake, half bird

The ancient Mesoamerican god Quetzalcóatl was known as the Feathered Serpent. He had the coils of a snake but also the feathers of the quetzal, a bird that lives in Mexico. Quetzals have bright, shimmering green feathers that ancient people loved to wear. Quetzalcóatl is often associated with being a ruler and having knowledge, and he plays an important role in many Aztec creation stories and myths.

Monster kids

Ancient Mesopotamian gods sometimes had children who turned out to be monstrous beasts. One of these was a demon called Lamashtu, who had the head of a lion. She was thrown out of the home of the gods when she told everyone that she wanted to eat human babies for dinner. Lamashtu roamed the Earth after that, stealing newborn babies and frightening pregnant women. This picture, made from volcanic glass, shows Lamashtu surrounded by objects associated with women—a comb, a pin, and a spindle used for weaving. They might have been given to her by women as offerings, in exchange for protection for themselves and their children.

Master of the Animals

The Master of Animals was a hero who was often shown in art by the Minoans of ancient Crete. We do not know whether the Minoans thought that he was a god who had the power to control animals, or a superhumanly strong hero who fought against animals until they gave him power over them. In this gold pendant, made around 1,850–1,550 BCE, he is holding two large birds.

Chief of the Sea

The Kwakwaka'wakw are an Indigenous people of the northwest coast of North America. Their ancestors made this mask (above) to show Komokwa, the Chief of the Sea, also called Kumugwe or Copper Maker. He was a powerful supernatural being. He ruled over all the creatures of the sea, including any land dwellers who fell in. The mask shows that Kumugwe looked like a sea creature himself, from his scalloped beard to the gills around his mouth.

THE MOUNTAIN SPIRIT AND THE DRAGON

Up high in the mountains, where the peaks were covered in snow, there lived a young nature spirit named Âu Cơ. It is not wrong to say that Âu Cơ lived in the mountain, but it would be more true to say that Âu Cơ was the mountain. Her hands were as cold to the touch as the peak of the mountain and wherever she went, she could not shake the feeling that she was very high up, even when she was walking on flat ground.

Although her heart belonged to the mountains, Âu Cơ often came down from the peaks and traveled far and wide. She loved to visit those who were sick, because she was particularly skilled at using plants to cure them. And although she missed the mountains while she was away, she knew that it would be wrong to keep the medicines that she made away from people who were ill.

One day while she was traveling back to her mountain home, she felt a tingle up the back of her spine that told her danger was close. A huge shadow was cast over the mountain and when she turned, an enormous fox with nine bushy tails was staring back at her, bearing her sharp, white teeth. Âu Cơ recognized her immediately—this was Hồ Tinh, the monster who had eaten all of the humans from the nearby villages. Now that there were no

humans left to eat, she had ventured further up the mountain in search of her next meal. Âu Cơ was trapped, and could think of no way out.

Suddenly, a huge wave rose from the sea below. From the top of the crest of the wave came Lạc Long Quân, who took the form of a dragon, and who Âu Cơ had heard stories about but had

Ceramic dragon, 15th century

Dragons are one of the most common images in Vietnamese art as well as appearing in myths. This dragon was hollow and used for pouring water.

never met. Lạc Long Quân flew through the air and circled around Hồ Tinh, but the fox monster was so huge and had such thick red fur that his sword alone could do nothing to harm her. The dragon god summoned the wind and the thunder to him and they too surrounded Hồ Tinh and made a storm that was so loud and so powerful that even the monster put each of her nine tails between her legs and ran back to her lair in fear. Âu Cơ thanked Lạc Long Quân and headed back up to the peak of the mountain as quickly as she could.

Safely inside her home on the peak of the mountain, Âu Cơ found that she could not stop thinking about Lạc Long Quân. Her feelings for him were huge and all-consuming, and felt like something more than gratitude to the water dragon god who had saved her life. Âu Cơ did not have any words to describe her emotions, but if she had been a human she would have called it "love." So she found it hard to hide how happy she felt when, the very next day, Lạc Long Quân made his way up the mountain to visit her, and asked her to marry him. She agreed, without needing to think too hard about it. Not long after they were married, she gave birth to a hundred scaly dragon eggs.

To the surprise of both of their parents, the children who hatched from the eggs were neither baby dragons nor mountain spirits, but took the shape of humans. The baby humans grew quickly, and soon they were crawling and toddling up and down the mountain between the sea where their water dragon father lived and the snowy peak that their mountain spirit mother called home. But the parents of these humans did not find living in two different places as easy as their babies seemed to. There was no way that they could live together, no matter how much they wanted to. Lạc Long Quân could not survive for very long outside of the water, and Âu Cơ could not imagine being separated from the mountains that were a part of everything she was.

Âu Cơ's heart was heavy and there were tears in her eyes when she told Lạc Long Quân that they could no longer be together. "It will never work," she said, between sobs, "you could not live at the top of the mountain, just as I could not live at the bottom of the sea." Lạc Long Quân felt a sadness unlike anything he had ever felt before, but he agreed that he could no more ask Âu Cơ to leave her home any more than she could ask him to leave his. They agreed that they would divide the children equally between them, with 50 of them living at the top of the mountain and 50 living at the bottom of the sea. They held each other close one last time before separating forever. And on that day, Lạc Long Quân created the tide of the sea, so that each day the tide was high he could come a little closer to the mountain spirit Âu Cơ who he would never forget he had loved.

PERSEPHONE AND DEMETER

Zeus, the king of the gods, and Demeter, the goddess of the harvest, had a daughter called Persephone. She liked to play outside in the fields, smelling the wildflowers that grew there. Most days she would go down to the meadow and fill her pockets with flowers to take home to her mother. But one day everything changed for her. She was wandering, as she often did, through the meadow when she felt a sudden chill in the air. She had not brought a shawl with her to wrap around herself and she shivered with cold. But it was not just the cold that was bothering her. She could not shake the feeling that something really very bad was about to happen. And she was right.

Out of nowhere, Hades, god of the Underworld, appeared. Hades was Zeus's brother, but Persephone did not think that this god and her father were at all alike. In fact, she hardly knew Hades at all, since she had lived on Earth her whole life and Hades lived down in the darkness of the Underworld. Persephone felt fear in the pit of her stomach and her instinct told her it was Hades. She started to run, but Hades was a powerful god and in a gust of cold air he summoned his chariot, pulled by four black horses galloping at full speed. The chariot caught up with Persephone before she had run even a few paces through the meadow.

Hades grabbed her by the
wrist and pulled her on board.
Persephone tried to call out for help, but there was
no one around to hear. The horses galloped on and
Hades took Persephone down to the Underworld with him.

Demeter was beginning to get worried. It was not like her daughter
to be out so late without leaving a note. She went to the meadow
to search for Persephone but found only a strange, cold mist that
chilled her to the bone. Full of fear, Demeter started to run. She ran
all over the world calling out for her daughter. As she ran, she
decreed that until she had found Persephone, there would be no
harvest, no crops, and no rain. The humans would have nothing
to eat until she was reunited with her daughter.

Eventually, the Sun took pity on Demeter and told her what had
happened. Demeter went straight to Zeus and told him, desperately,
that their daughter had been kidnapped. Zeus was upset but not
sure that anything could be done—the two brothers were equal in
their powers, except that Zeus ruled over the land of the living and
Hades ruled over the land of the dead. If Persephone had gone
beyond the land of the living, Zeus was not sure that he could get
her back.

Before long, the humans began to complain loudly about the fact that they did not have any food. They prayed to the gods to bring an end to the famine that they were suffering. Seeing the humans so upset made Zeus relent, and he told Demeter that it might be possible for Persephone to come back to the land of the living as long as—this part was crucial, he explained—she had not eaten a single mouthful of food while she was there. Demeter did not understand why this was the case, but she did not have time to argue. She needed to find Persephone before she got hungry and ate something.

Demeter could feel the presence of her daughter as soon as she entered the Underworld. Among all of the darkness and gloom in the land of the dead, Persephone had brought light and flowers. But Persephone was not happy here. As soon as she caught sight of her mother, she ran toward her with tears in her eyes. Demeter thought for a moment that she looked like a child even though she was almost a young woman. Persephone started to tell her mother what had happened but

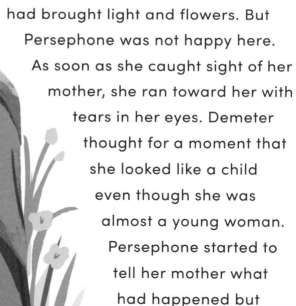

Demeter stopped her. "All I need to know," Demeter said, sounding nervous, "is whether you have eaten any food while you have been here." Persephone looked at her in confusion. "Only a few pomegranate seeds," she said. "What difference does it make?"

At this, Demeter started to cry, too. Taking her daughter's hand, she made her way to the palace at the center of the Underworld and pleaded with Hades to release Persephone. Hades refused. He enjoyed the flowers and the brightness that Persephone brought with her. But he was also more concerned than he would admit about what Zeus would say when he found out that Hades had imprisoned his daughter. He offered Demeter a compromise. Persephone would spend half of the year in the land of the living with her mother, and the other half in the Underworld with Hades. Demeter and Persephone had no choice but to accept.

Eventually, the whole of the world accepted it, too. In the six months that Persephone spent in the land of the living, flowers would bloom and the sun would shine, and humans would plant crops to grow. When the time came for Persephone to return to the Underworld's cold, a wet mist would fall over the world, the leaves would fall from the trees, and all of the plants and flowers would wither and die. On Earth the humans would call the time when Persephone was in the Underworld "winter," and when she returned to the land of the living "spring."

GODS OF THE SEASONS

Human beings have always been reliant on the seasons and good weather for growing food. Ancient people prayed to gods that they believed controlled the cycles of nature. The Bugkalot people of the Philippines prayed to the god Oden for rain, Persian mythology spoke of Nane Sarma ("Grandma Snow"), while the Inuit people called on the goddess Asiaq to melt the snow and send the spring. The changing color of the leaves in fall was thought to be the work of gods and goddesses, too, with Papa Bois responsible for the forests in some ancient African (and later Caribbean) myths.

Harvest bells

In ancient Japan, bells called dōtaku were used in ceremonies for bringing a good harvest. Around the third century BCE, Japanese people changed from mostly eating animals that they hunted, to eating food that they farmed, especially rice. Festivals took place every year when the rice seeds had been planted. People prayed to the gods of the harvest, asking them to make the crops grow. After the festival the dōtaku bells were buried in the ground to absorb the life force of the Earth before being used again. They belonged to the community as a whole and not to any one person.

Nature spirit

The coming of spring and the fertility of crops was a hugely important event in the lives of many ancient people, many of whom lived only from what the land provided them. This object shows an Indian nature spirit called a yaksha. These spirits could be kind and helpful or mischievous and hurtful. They were associated with crops, trees, and spring. Yakshas were local gods and goddesses, and many towns would have had their own yaksha who they got to know well.

Gods of the flood

In ancient Egypt, the flooding of the Nile was the most important event, and made all of life possible for the people who lived on the river's banks. Although we now know that the flood comes because of snow melting in the mountains, the ancient Egyptians thought the gods did it. They thanked Hapi, the god of the floods, and also believed that Taweret, the goddess of childbirth, was in part responsible for it. This statue shows Taweret, who had the head of a hippo.

Prayer for help

Ancient people knew exactly what would help their crops grow: sunlight and rain. Ancient Mesopotamia had plenty of both (this area is called "the Fertile Crescent" for this reason). The people there gave thanks to the gods for their lucky place in the world—and asked for help when they needed it. Art often showed people, like this young man, raising plants up toward the sun (which was often shown flying in the sky with wings) and asking the gods and goddesses to help him.

Dragons were one of the first images ever to appear in Chinese art. This dragon pendant was made from precious jade around 3,500 BCE.

Dragon of day and night

In Chinese mythology day and night is caused by a huge dragon called Zhulong. When he opens his eyes it is daylight, and when he closes them darkness falls. It is also Zhulong who can summon wind and rain. This god does not need to breathe like humans do, but myth says that when he does, his breath creates winds. When he blows air it is cold winter, and when he breathes out air it is hot summer.

Spirits of rain

In the Dogon religion, spirits help crops grow and people to have children. The Dogon people lived in a very dry area and so they really needed the help of the spirits. They made statues of humans worshipping spirits and left them at special shrines. The statues were often made of wood, a material that usually rots away, but was preserved in this region because the air is so dry. The figure in this wooden statue is raising their arms to ask the spirits to send rain.

KEEPING HUMANS IN LINE

Many of the stories that ancient people told about their gods and goddesses were about the ways they punished humans who disobeyed them. Gods and goddesses set strict rules and limits for humans, and they did not like it when they challenged their opinions, or boasted about their own power, or tried to take control of things that were not for humans to control. These stories are often scary and had grisly endings, but they allowed humans to decide on rules to live by, hoping to avoid the fate of those who angered the gods.

ANANSI AND THE WISDOM OF THE WORLD

Nyame the sky god had given Anansi the spider a very special task. The god had called out to the scuttling creature and asked him to collect together all of the wisdom in the world, bring it up into the sky, and give it to him. If Anansi agreed to do this, Nyame promised that he would give him something very special in return. But Anansi was not so naïve as to carry out the task before he had found out what the reward would be. "And if I do it, what will you give me?" he asked Nyame. Nyame thought about this for a moment, and then he spoke. "If you do it, I will give you a glittering crown to wear on your head." Anansi did not seem convinced. "And on the crown," Nyame continued, "I will write the

words 'The Cleverest Creature in All the World' so that everyone who you pass in the street will know who you are." At this, Anansi's six eyes lit up, and he agreed to do as the sky god had asked.

Nyame chuckled to himself, knowing that he had found the spider's weakness. Anansi did not hear him, though—because he was busy chuckling to himself, too. Anansi was delighted to have been given such an easy task. In his own mind, he was sure that he already knew everything there was to know in the world. In fact, he had been collecting knowledge and wisdom from everyone he met for as long as he could remember. He had stored it in a pot made from the skin of a calabash, in a hole he had dug in his garden. It would take him no time at all to dig it up and to deliver it to the sky god. Nyame, he was sure, would hardly be able to believe how quickly he had accomplished his task.

Anansi went back home and dug up the calabash pot from his garden. His wife Aso was not convinced of his plan. "Are you absolutely sure," she asked him, "that the sky god Nyame would give you such a simple task?" But Anansi did not listen. He was impatient to get his hands on the glittering crown that would announce to everyone that he was the cleverest creature in all the world. He carried the calabash pot with all of the wisdom of the world inside it through the village. He moved slowly because the pot was heavy—which was hardly surprising given the weight of all the wisdom it contained.

Eventually, Anansi arrived at the tallest palm
trees in the village, the one that he had heard
other people say they had used to climb all
the way up into the sky where Nyame lived.
He tied the calabash pot to his back so that
all eight of his legs were free to climb. Then,
slowly but surely, he began to climb to the
treetops. By the time he reached the level
of the rooftops, a crowd was starting
to gather at the bottom of the tree.
Humans were watching the spider climb
with the enormous calabash pot on his
back. And they were cheering him on,
beating drums in time with the movement
of his legs and shouting out encouraging
words. "Look at that spider!" one of
them shouted, and "What a clever
creature!" said another.

When Anansi heard this, he stopped climbing
for a moment and turned his head around so
he could see which of the humans it was
who had recognized his cleverness at
last. He lifted up one of his eight legs
to wave to them.

The crowd of humans below cheered so he lifted another, and then another. Suddenly, he began to feel a strange sensation, almost like he was falling at speed from a great height, and realized he had let go of the trunk of the palm tree completely. Anansi landed with a thud in the dust and when he opened his six eyes, he saw each of the humans who had been cheering only moments ago gazing at him from above, with a mixture of worry and disappointment on their faces.

The calabash pot had shattered into small pieces all around him and all of the wisdom and knowledge that he had collected together had escaped from the pot. It made its way first around the village, into the homes of all of the humans, and then across all of the rest of the world. From the sky, Anansi heard a rumbling that sounded a little like thunder—Nyame was laughing. "So you didn't have all of the knowledge in the world then, Anansi! After all, if you knew all that there is to know, you would surely have known not to lift your legs from the trunk of a palm tree when you are trying to climb it." Nyame laughed again. Anansi learned that day that he would never know everything there was to know. But although his pride was dented, he soon returned to trying to be the cleverest creature in the whole world.

HI'IAKA TEACHES PAPULEHU A LESSON

The goddess Hi'iaka was born in unusual circumstances. Her mother did not give birth to her, but instead laid her in an egg. The egg was carried to Hawai'i by Hi'iaka's older sister, Pele. Pele kept the egg close to her body for the whole journey to keep it warm. When they arrived, the egg hatched and the two sisters grew up together. Pele became the goddess of volcanoes, and Hi'iaka became the goddess of magic and medicine. They were happy enough, though Pele could never leave the island because if she did, no one would be able to keep the volcanoes under control.

When they got older, Hi'iaka fell in love with a human woman called Hopoe, who taught her how to string flowers together so that she could wear them around her neck. Hi'iaka and Hopoe made their home together in a forest of lehua trees not far from the volcano where Pele lived. Pele, on the other hand, had never met anyone she thought she might fall in love with. But all of that changed on the day that Lohi'au arrived. Lohi'au was a singer, and as soon as Pele heard his beautiful voice echoing all across the island, she knew that she had fallen in love.

As quickly as he had arrived, Lohi'au was gone again, back to his home on a little island just across the sea. Pele was devastated

that he had left, and even more devastated by the fact that she could not go and find him because she could not leave the island. She asked Hi'iaka to go to the island where Lohi'au lived and bring him back with her so that she could marry him. Hi'iaka agreed, even though she knew how dangerous the journey would be.

Pele gave her sister three gifts to help her on her journey. First, she gave her eyes the ability to see into the future. Then she gave her arms a special strength so that she could fight any enemies she met on her way. Then she gave her a skirt that she had woven out of leaves and lightning so that she would always be able to summon a storm if she needed to. Hi'iaka put on the skirt and set off.

Pele was right—Hi'iaka would need all the help that she could get. She trekked through forests so thick she could not see her own feet and crossed mountains and deep rivers. At every turn she fought off terrifying monsters who could change their shape at a moment's notice. Each time she escaped them by summoning a storm with her lightning skirt or using her strong arms to fight them off. She did not think about stopping or turning back, not even once.

It was only when Hiʻiaka came across the palace of princess Papulehu that she stopped to rest. The princess was kind and welcoming, and gave her garlands of flowers to wear around her neck. At first, she reminded Hiʻiaka a little of Hopoe, the woman she had left behind at home in the forest. But as she stayed longer, it became obvious to Hiʻiaka that something was wrong. Papulehu, it seemed, did not pray to the gods.

When Hiʻiaka asked her about it, Papulehu said that she could not see the point in praying when she already had everything that she could wish for. "What does a princess need to ask the gods for?" she asked. Hiʻiaka decided she needed to teach the princess a lesson. It was goddesses like her who had given Papulehu such an easy life and they could just as easily take it away again. So when Hiʻiaka foresaw—using the magical power that her sister had given her—that the next day a moʻo would come to the palace disguised as a lizard, she decided not to warn Papulehu.

The moʻo were powerful beings that could disguise themselves so that they looked just like the ordinary lizards that scuttled around the palace floor. But the moʻo were not like ordinary lizards. Some people said that they were the spirits of people who had long ago died. And others said that they could curse—or even eat—human beings. The most frightening thing of all about them, was that it was impossible for any human to know whether a lizard was just an ordinary lizard or a moʻo in disguise.

The next day, Papulehu was wandering down the hallway in her palace when a tiny lizard scuttled across the floor and stopped in front of her. Papulehu thought nothing of it—there were many lizards in the palace. But all of a sudden it changed, becoming a huge reptile with enormous teeth, and swallowed her whole.

Papulehu screamed from inside the creature's stomach, but it was no good—the mo'o's scaly skin was too thick and no one could hear her. No one, that is, except Hi'iaka, who had stayed close by. Using her magically strong arms, she wrestled the mo'o to the ground. Then she spoke to Papulehu, leaning in close to the creature's belly. "I will release you only if you promise to pray to the gods and goddess and never to take your happy life for granted ever again!" Papulehu agreed instantly. Hi'iaka wrapped her arms around the mo'o and squeezed with all of her strength—and Papulehu came out the same way she had gone in.

Eventually, Hi'iaka found Lohi'au's island and took him back to the volcano where her sister lived. She returned to Hopoe and their home in the forest of lehua trees. And although she did not see Papulehu ever again, she knew that the princess would respect the gods and would no longer take any of the good things in her life for granted.

ATHENA LOSES HER TEMPER

The goddess Athena was well known as the best weaver on Mount Olympus, where all of the gods and goddesses lived. So you can imagine how surprised she was to hear one day about a young human girl from Lydia who claimed to have even greater skill. This girl, named Arachne, had been telling everyone who would listen that she was better at weaving than even the goddess Athena. Athena could not put up with this. She went down into the human world immediately to find Arachne and remind the young girl that it was Athena who was the goddess of arts and crafts.

Athena found Arachne in a place that was unlike anything she had expected. She had imagined that the girl would be sitting behind an enormous loom, with wool all of the colors of the rainbow ready for her to weave into beautiful creations. She had expected to find the daughter of a king or a queen, or perhaps even the child of some god or goddess who had given her special powers. But Arachne was a very ordinary sort of a person who lived in a small house with her father. When Athena found her she was busy carding wool and turning it from a fluffy cloud into a finely spun thread, sitting all by herself. Athena disguised herself as an old woman and knocked on the door.

When Arachne answered, the goddess pretended to be a passer-by who had stopped to offer the girl some friendly advice. "Listen to some wise words, girl, from an old woman who has your best interests at heart," she said. "Do not go around telling everyone that you are a better weaver than a goddess herself! Surely you must have misspoken. Say that you are a mere human and your skills are but an echo of those of the goddess. Ask Athena to forgive you, and I am sure that she will do so." But Arachne believed in her talent and did not appreciate the old woman's advice. "Why have you come to my house to tell me what to do?" she asked, with anger in her voice. "If Athena is so worried about what I have said, she should come here herself and challenge me to a weaving competition!"

The moment she heard Arachne's words, Athena dropped her disguise, revealing herself as a goddess. She challenged Arachne to the competition as she had suggested. Immediately, they set about their work, Arachne at her loom and Athena next to her. They worked late into the evening and through the night and they did not stop weaving until dawn crept across the sky again the next day. Arachne's eyes were closing with tiredness, but goddesses do not grow tired the way that humans do, so Athena was able to sneak a glance at the tapestry that Arachne had made. The goddess realized that she could not say that her own tapestry was better than this human girl's. Arachne had woven each of the gods of Mount Olympus so skilfully that Athena could tell immediately which was which. There was no other way to put it: Arachne was a better weaver than the goddess Athena herself—and that, Athena could not stand.

In a sudden rage, Athena tore Arachne's weaving in two, straight down the middle. Arachne was terrified of the goddess's anger, but Athena was only just getting started. Once she had torn Arachne's tapestry to pieces, she turned on the human girl herself. "So, you want to be a better weaver even than a goddess? Then weave your web for as long as you live." And with that, she tapped Arachne on the forehead with the shuttle from her loom. Arachne's hair fell out of her head onto the floor next to her. From her armpits and her hips an extra set of arms and legs grew until she had eight limbs all together. Her human form was gone entirely and her body shrunk until it was so tiny that she was afraid Athena might step on her. Arachne had become a spider. Now, instead of weaving beautiful tapestries, she would spend the rest of her life weaving the web that she would call home. Although none of the other humans in Lydia thought that Athena's treatment of the girl was fair, they never again boasted that they were better than a god or a goddess at anything at all.

SEKHMET'S REVENGE

The sun god Ra had overheard the humans plotting against him. "Who does he think he is, stealing the Sun from us every night and only bringing it back hours later in the morning?" they whispered to each other. Ra, who saw and heard everything that happened on Earth, was furious. He expected the humans to be grateful that he gave them the sunlight that lit up their homes and made their crops grow tall and strong in the fields. He decided to punish them.

Years ago, when his daughter Sekhmet had been born, Ra had given her a name that made her perfectly suited for punishing humans. "Sekhmet" in the ancient Egyptian language meant "The Powerful One," and he had also given his daughter nicknames like "The One Evil Trembles Before" and "Queen of Dread." Sekhmet lived up to these names. The humans were terrified of Sekhmet, and said that when she was angry she breathed a fire that could burn down whole villages, and sent plagues that no human could survive. Ra had never had reason to depend on his daughter's viciousness for anything before, but he made a plan to punish the humans and placed his daughter Sekhmet right at the center of it.

Sekhmet was the goddess of war and she had the head of a lion—but when her father told her what he had overheard the humans whispering, she quickly transformed the rest of her body into the body of a lioness, too. She prowled her way to the Earth and roared so loudly that all of the humans ran out of their villages to try to escape her. But none of them were fast enough. Sekhmet hunted down the humans and killed those she could find. She did not feel sorry for the humans, because feeling sorry for humans was not among her powers. Even if she had hesitated, she would simply have reminded herself of the way that the humans had disrespected her father the sun god, and continued on her rampage.

So much human blood was spilled as the goddess took her revenge that the Nile River ran red. Sekhmet stuck out her tongue like a cat crouched over a bowl of milk and lapped it up. Ra, who was watching all of this happen, began to wonder whether there would be any humans left at all when Sekhmet had finished. The sky grew darker than usual because Ra did not like to watch all of this violence take place and withdrew from the land into the sky to distance himself from it. Ra called out to his daughter to stop killing the humans but she did not listen. In fact, Ra was not even sure if she could hear him or whether she was so focused on the scent of blood that she did not even know he was calling to her.

Ra realized that he would have to find a way to stop Sekhmet. He squeezed the juice from hundreds of pomegranate fruits. He mixed the juice with a strong beer that was famous across ancient Egypt, because

anyone who drank it fell asleep almost instantly. The pomegranate juice stained the beer red so that it looked just like human blood. Then he poured it over the fields between the village that Sekhmet had just prowled out of and the village she was about to arrive at. As Sekhmet crossed the fields, she was surprised to find that the humans had already been killed—or at least, so it seemed, because the fields were stained with red human blood. She lapped up all of the blood and immediately fell into a deep sleep.

When she awoke, Ra explained to her that he had changed his mind and no longer wanted her to kill all of the humans. Coming back to her senses, Sekhmet agreed that the humans had suffered enough and that they had learned a harsh lesson—and both Sekhmet and Ra were sure that the humans would not be so disrespectful of the gods ever again. The sun god would never fully trust the humans in the same way again, though, and moved far away from the Earth, leaving the human world a little darker. On cloudy days or when they were struggling to see in the evenings, the humans would remember to be grateful for Ra the sun god, who came back and brought them light every morning.

Stone sculpture, c. 664–332 BCE

Statues of the goddess Sekhmet were carved to look intimidating. This reminded people to give her offerings so she would not go on any more rampages.

VENGEFUL GODS AND EVIL SPIRITS

Gods and goddesses in the ancient world were not always kind and good. They could also be frightening! Ancient people had to try to stay on the right side of them. Before science could explain things like diseases, people thought that feeling unwell or just plain bad luck meant they had angered the gods. Many ancient people carried objects that they used to ward off evil spirits or gave offerings to the gods and goddesses to protect themselves from their anger.

Egyptian protector god

Many ancient Egyptians worshipped the god Bes, who they hoped would protect them from evil spirits that caused people to become ill and die. He particularly watched over children and babies, and liked to make them laugh. Bes was worshipped in other parts of ancient Africa like Somalia and Nubia, too. This object shows Bes in the form of a man who has dwarfism. He wears the mane of a lion and a plumed crown.

Keep an eye out

Gifts are a good way to keep temperamental gods happy. In ancient Syria there was a temple in a city called Tell Brak. When modern-day archaeologists started to dig around the temple, they found thousands of mysterious figurines with huge eyes. It is still unclear exactly what all of these little statues were used for, but archaeologists think that they might have been left as offerings to appease angry gods.

Music and magic

Ancient Egyptians carried a type of rattle called a sistrum (right). Their instruments made a soothing noise to calm the anger of gods or goddesses toward the humans who crossed their path. The ancient Romans used similar rattles in their religious ceremonies, but theirs were not for soothing. The sistrum made a jingling noise that the Romans believed would scare away evil spirits.

This sistrum is decorated with the head of the goddess Hathor. According to myth, she was a grumpy goddess and the other goddesses danced to sistrum music to try and cure her bad moods.

Fierce protector

Humbaba was an enormous demon in the ancient Mesopotamian religion. He could breathe fire, cause floods by roaring, and was put on Earth by the god Enlil to terrify the humans and to stop them from entering the cedar forest and stealing valuable timber. Plaques like this one, showing the head of Humbaba, were often fixed to doorways and gates. People hoped Humbaba would protect their homes the way he protected the forest and would stop anyone with evil intentions from entering the building. Humbaba was killed by Gilgamesh and Enkidu, who took timber from the cedar forest back with them to the city of Uruk. The story is told in an ancient poem called *The Epic of Gilgamesh*, which is sometimes called the first ever work of literature.

Warlike goddess

The gods and goddesses that humans asked for help were often as threatening toward their own followers as they were toward their enemies. This goddess is fierce—it would be better to be her friend than her enemy! Her hair is bristling with weapons like axes and spears. Images of ferocious goddesses like this were made in the ancient city of Pataliputra in India.

THE PRINCE AND THE MOON

There was once a king who was excellent in all things, except for the fact that he could never say no to his son. The little prince only had to mention a new toy and it would appear in front of him, or look in the direction of the kitchen and a banquet would be laid out before him. By the time he was 10, the prince was tired of all of the things he could think of to ask for.

To keep him busy, all the children in the kingdom had to play with the prince from morning until evening and had no choice but to agree. Eventually, one young girl became fed up with playing these games that she did not want to play. "I can think of something that your father cannot give you," she told the prince. He laughed and told her that his father was the most powerful man in the world and could give him anything. "Not quite anything," she replied. "He cannot give you

the Moon." For a moment the prince did not know what to say. All of the other children began to laugh. The prince blushed with embarrassment, and he ran to the palace to tell his father to give him the Moon immediately. His father smiled and shook his head, but the prince insisted. "I want the Moon, father. You are the most powerful man in the world, surely you will give it to me?" The king promised to come up with a plan. He summoned his royal advisors, but when he explained to them what his son had asked, they began to shift awkwardly in their seats. "No one can take the Moon from the sky, great king," one of them said tentatively. The king ordered them to find a way.

The advisors were in an impossible position. Even if they could have managed it, they were sure that the gods would punish them for taking down the Moon. But if they did nothing, they would be punished by the king. They sat all night discussing the matter. The next morning one of the advisors, an older woman from a neighboring village, had a plan. "What if it was not us who took the Moon from the sky, but the prince himself?" The king agreed and sent a message out to all of the villages in the kingdom, asking them to send their best builders. They were going to build a tower.

Every day while the work was taking place, the prince brought the girl who had taunted him to watch the tower being built. "Don't do this, prince," she said, when she saw how high the tower was. "You do not need to prove anything to me, I don't want you to get hurt." But the prince did not listen. As soon as it was finished, he started to climb up the tower and he called to the king to join him – the king, of course, agreed. They started to climb up and up until they were so close to the Moon that it was the only thing they could see.

When they were close enough to touch the Moon, the prince stretched out his hand, but jumped backward so suddenly that he almost fell from the very top of the tower. The Moon was hot and it burned him. The piece of the Moon he had touched broke off in his hand and he dropped it onto the wooden planks of the tower, which caught fire immediately. The tower burned quickly and the people who had gathered below started to run in all directions. The girl who had taunted the prince had not dared to come out to watch him climb the tower, but stood at her bedroom window gazing in horror as the flames spread down to the bottom of it.

The gods, who had been watching this charade all along from the sky, shook their heads. They began to argue over what should be done. Some felt that these silly humans deserved their fate and wanted to leave them to be burned to a crisp along with the wooden tower. Others felt some pity and said that the humans couldn't help their silliness and should not be punished for it. In her bedroom, standing by the window, the girl who had taunted the prince was praying and asking the gods to forgive him for wanting the Moon. And although the prince and the king were not aware of it yet, the gods had heard her prayer.

As the tower crumbled in the flames, the king and his son leaped up into the air and found to their surprise that they did not fall down to the ground as they had expected. They floated, or rather, they flew, because the gods had turned them into birds that could swoop through the sky. The prince and the king survived, but they would never return to their human form again. And whenever the people of the kingdom saw birds flying overhead, it would remind them not to want impossible things and to be grateful for what they have.

SUPERHUMANS

Most people in the ancient world felt like they were completely under the power of gods and goddesses. The creation of the world and the power over life and death belonged to the gods, so humans had to do their best to stay on the right side of them. However, some unusual humans were more like the gods and goddesses than others. Ancient myths from all over the world tell stories of humans who were capable of extraordinary things, and wielded such power that they could even compete with the gods.

Ancient Greek vases for holding wine or water were called "amphorae." This one shows Herakles fighting the Hydra, a monster with many heads.

Bull tamer

Ancient people who tamed large, dangerous animals like bulls were said to have superhuman skills. This statue of a bull was made around 5,000 years ago by ancient people who lived along the Indus River Valley, an area that today covers North India and Pakistan. Ancient Indus Valley art also often shows supermen and superwomen taming bulls.

Herakles the hero

The ancient Greeks told many stories about the adventures of their brave human or half-human heroes. One of their most famous heroes was Herakles. He was half-human, half-god, the son of the king of the gods, Zeus, and a woman called Alcmene. Herakles was tormented by the goddess Hera and eventually tasked with completing 12 "labors," dangerous and difficult tasks that no ordinary human would be capable of. When Herakles died, the gods rewarded him by making him a full god.

Hypatia

Some superhumans were famous for their cleverness and knowledge. Hypatia was a mathematician and philosopher who lived in Egypt in the fourth century. She was praised far and wide for her ability to calculate difficult sums using algebra. She was one of the world's greatest astronomers, mapping the stars in the sky.

Superbabies

The Olmec people of ancient Mexico made a lot of art that featured supernatural babies. These babies look realistic, but the artists have also made them slightly superhuman. They have tattoos on their bodies and wear ceremonial headdresses (painted red or pink in this statue). We do not know whether these statues are supposed to represent the spirits of babies who left the world of the living too early, or the divine power of new life on Earth. But it is clear from the statues that the Olmec people considered these babies to be more powerful than ordinary humans.

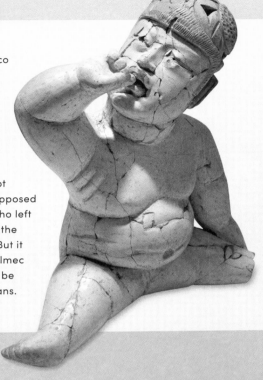

Special bonds

Not all of the special humans recorded in ancient art were superhuman or heroic. Families were very important to the ancient Egyptians, so people kept statues in their homes of their close family members (right). This family group (left) was captured in a statue around 2455–2350 BCE. It includes Nykara, center, who was the chief of the granary. He may have had this statue made to commemorate his family. Many ancient cultures valued the bonds between family members as some of the strongest forces in the world.

A WORLD OF GODS

All across the ancient world, people told stories about gods and goddesses to make sense of the world around them. Some of those gods and goddesses died with the people who worshipped them back then, but some of them are with us still, worshipped by the distant descendants of those ancient people. And around the world new gods have joined them, in religions that did not yet exist in ancient times.

We all believe in something. Perhaps you call the thing that you believe in a god, either one god or many gods. Or perhaps you call it something different, like a philosophy or a theory. Perhaps you would say—if someone were to ask you—that you don't believe in anything at all. But you are nonetheless convinced that the Sun will rise tomorrow morning, just as it rose this morning and has risen every day for as long as you can remember. You are sure that this is what will happen based on your experience of the world, even though you don't know for certain that it will always be true. That is a belief.

Beliefs can be complicated. We can find ourselves arguing about them even when we aren't sure why we are arguing, even with people we love very much. Humans don't tell stories because they are easy or simple. They turn to myths because something is hard to understand or hurts to think about. Myths offer us a very special kind of knowledge—they aren't concerned with being true in any real or scientific sense. But they give us a way of understanding and coming to terms with the things we experience. When we look at the stories that ancient people told all over the world and the gods and goddesses they believed in, we can see that we are all much more similar in our hopes and our fears than we might otherwise think. For most of history, we humans have all been asking very similar questions about the world in which we live.

There are huge differences between how different
groups of ancient people honored their gods.
Some of them prayed, sang songs, danced, and
wrote poems for their gods, while others made
sacrifices, giving up something that meant a lot to
them to show how much they cared. Some gods were
dangerous and demanding, and humans feared harsh
punishment if they did not obey them. Other gods did
not ask for very much from their human worshippers
at all, and simply lived alongside them as friends.

But even with all of these differences, gods taught
humans very similar core values, wherever in the world
they were (or still are) worshipped. They taught them not to
be proud or to boast, to be grateful for the things that the gods
provided for them, and not to waste their lives wanting things they
could not have, whether that is money or the Moon. They taught
them to be kind, to behave honestly with each other, and to be gentle
guardians of the Earth. And even those people who do not believe in
any god or gods at all could not deny that they have some of the
values that these stories taught to ancient people all those years ago.

INDEX

ACKNOWLEDGMENTS

DK would like to thank: Eleanor Home (MPhil), Dr. Karen Jacobs, Dr. Ellie Mackin Roberts, Dr. Justine McConnell, Aasha (DK India's Diversity, Equity, & Inclusion team), Dr. Dana Healy, Prof. David Carrasco, Prof. Almut Hintze FBA, Charles Y. Kwong, Dr. Marie Rodet, and Timothy Topper, M.Ed.